GENERATIVE AI FOR RETAIL INDUSTRY

Rakesh Kumar

Dedicated to all the innovative minds and forward-thinking leaders in the retail industry who are embracing the power of Generative AI to transform the shopping experience. Your dedication to pushing boundaries and exploring new frontiers is shaping the future of retail, paving the way for a more personalized, efficient, and delightful shopping journey for customers around the world.

CONTENTS

INTRODUCTION

Welcome to "Generative AI for Retail Industry," where we embark on a journey through the intersection of artificial intelligence and retail innovation. In this book, we delve into the transformative potential of Generative AI technologies and their profound impact on the retail landscape.

The retail industry is undergoing a remarkable evolution, driven by advancements in technology and changing consumer expectations. Today's consumers demand personalized experiences, seamless interactions, and unparalleled convenience. To meet these demands and stay ahead in an increasingly competitive market, retailers are turning to Generative AI – a cutting-edge branch of artificial intelligence that enables machines to generate new content, designs, and solutions autonomously.

Generative AI holds immense promise for revolutionizing various aspects of the retail industry, from product design and customer engagement to supply chain optimization and beyond. By harnessing the power of deep learning, neural networks, and advanced algorithms, retailers can unlock new possibilities for enhancing customer experiences, driving operational efficiencies, and unlocking business growth.

In this book, we explore the diverse applications of Generative AI across the retail ecosystem, providing insights, case studies, and practical examples to illustrate how this transformative technology is reshaping the future of retail. From personalized product recommendations and virtual try-on experiences to dynamic pricing strategies and supply chain optimization, we uncover the myriad ways in which Generative AI is driving innovation and creating value for retailers and consumers alike.

Whether you're a retail executive seeking to stay ahead of the curve, a technologist exploring the latest AI trends, or an entrepreneur looking to disrupt the retail landscape, this book offers valuable insights and actionable strategies to leverage Generative AI for success in the dynamic world of retail.

Join us as we embark on a journey of discovery, exploration, and innovation, as we unlock the full potential of Generative AI to revolutionize the retail industry and shape the future of commerce.

UNDERSTANDING GENERATIVE AI

Generative AI refers to a subset of artificial intelligence (AI) techniques that focus on generating new data or content that is similar to, but not the same as, existing data. Unlike traditional AI models that are designed for tasks such as classification, prediction, or decision-making based on given input data, generative AI models are trained to create new data samples that have similar characteristics to the training data.

The primary goal of generative AI is to enable machines to understand and create content that resembles what humans produce. This can include generating images, text, audio, video, or even entire virtual environments. Generative AI models often rely on deep learning techniques, particularly generative neural networks such as Generative Adversarial Networks (GANs), Variational Autoencoders (VAEs), and flow-based models.

Generative AI has applications across various domains, including:

1. Image Generation: Creating new images that resemble real photographs or artwork, which can be used for tasks like image synthesis, style transfer, and image-to-image translation.

2. Text Generation: Generating human-like text, such as articles, stories, dialogue, and poetry. Text generation models can be used for content creation, language translation, and natural language understanding tasks.

3. Music and Audio Generation: Creating new musical

compositions or generating audio samples that mimic human voices or environmental sounds.

4. Video Generation: Generating new video sequences, including animations, deepfakes, and video prediction.

5. Content Creation and Design: Generating designs, artwork, and creative content for applications in graphic design, advertising, and virtual environments.

Generative AI has seen rapid advancement in recent years, driven by improvements in deep learning algorithms, computational power, and the availability of large datasets. It holds promise for revolutionizing various industries by enabling more creative and personalized applications, enhancing user experiences, and automating content generation tasks. However, it also raises ethical concerns related to the potential misuse of generated content, privacy issues, and biases inherent in the training data.

EVOLUTION OF GENERATIVE MODELS

The historical evolution of generative models spans several decades, with significant advancements occurring in recent years due to breakthroughs in deep learning. Here's a brief overview:

1. Early Approaches:
   - Markov Chains: One of the earliest methods for generating sequences of data, such as text or music, based on probabilistic models.
   - Hidden Markov Models (HMMs): Used for modeling sequential data with hidden states, commonly applied in speech recognition and natural language processing.

2. Probabilistic Models:
   - Restricted Boltzmann Machines (RBMs): Introduced in the 1980s, RBMs are stochastic neural networks used for modeling probability distributions over binary-valued data. They formed the basis for later generative models.
   - Gaussian Mixture Models (GMMs): Probabilistic models used for clustering and density estimation, often applied in speech recognition and computer vision.

3. Variational Methods:
   - Variational Autoencoders (VAEs): Introduced in 2013, VAEs combine variational inference with neural network-based autoencoders to learn probabilistic representations of input data. They are capable of generating new samples by sampling from the learned latent space.

4. Adversarial Learning:

- Generative Adversarial Networks (GANs): Proposed in 2014, GANs consist of two neural networks, a generator and a discriminator, trained adversarially to generate realistic data samples. GANs have achieved remarkable success in generating high-quality images, text, and other data types.

5. Flow-Based Models:

- Normalizing Flows: A class of models introduced to learn invertible transformations between data distributions, allowing for efficient sampling and density estimation. Examples include RealNVP and Glow.

6. Hybrid Models and Extensions:

- Conditional Generative Models: Variants of generative models that condition the generation process on additional information, such as class labels or attributes.

- Progressive Growing of GANs (PGGANs): A technique for training GANs that involves incrementally adding layers to both the generator and discriminator, resulting in higher-resolution and more detailed output images.

7. Continual Advances:

- BigGAN: A variant of GANs designed for generating high-fidelity images using large-scale models and parallelism.

- StyleGAN: Introduced in 2018, StyleGAN improved upon previous GAN architectures by incorporating style-based generator networks, enabling more fine-grained control over generated images' appearance.

Throughout this evolution, generative models have become increasingly powerful and versatile, enabling applications across various domains such as computer vision, natural language processing, and creative content generation. Ongoing research continues to push the boundaries of generative AI, exploring new architectures, training techniques, and applications.

APPLICATIONS OF GENERATIVE AI IN VARIOUS INDUSTRIES

Generative AI has a wide range of applications across various industries, revolutionizing how businesses operate and interact with customers. Here are some examples of how generative AI is being applied in different sectors:

1. Retail:
   - Product Image Generation: Generative AI can create high-quality product images for e-commerce platforms, reducing the need for expensive photoshoots.
   - Virtual Try-On: Customers can virtually try on clothing, accessories, or makeup using augmented reality powered by generative models.
   - Personalized Marketing: AI-generated content can be tailored to individual customers based on their preferences and browsing history.

2. Healthcare:
   - Medical Image Synthesis: Generative models can generate synthetic medical images for training and augmenting datasets, aiding in the development of diagnostic tools and treatment planning.
   - Drug Discovery: AI-generated molecular structures can be used to design new drugs and predict their properties, accelerating the drug discovery process.

- Patient Data Augmentation: Synthetic patient data can be generated to augment real-world datasets, preserving privacy while enabling more comprehensive analysis and model training.

3. Entertainment:
- Content Creation: Generative AI is used to create music, art, and literature, providing new tools for artists and creators to explore innovative ideas and styles.
- Video Games: Procedural content generation techniques powered by generative models can create diverse and immersive game worlds, enhancing gameplay experiences.

4. Finance:
- Fraud Detection: Generative models can generate synthetic transaction data to train fraud detection algorithms, improving their accuracy and robustness.
- Portfolio Management: AI-generated forecasts and simulations can help investors optimize their portfolios and make informed decisions in dynamic financial markets.

5. Manufacturing:
- Generative Design: AI-generated designs and prototypes can optimize product performance and efficiency, reducing manufacturing costs and time-to-market.
- Predictive Maintenance: Generative models can predict equipment failures and maintenance needs based on sensor data, minimizing downtime and maximizing productivity.

6. Marketing and Advertising:
- Content Generation: AI-generated content, such as ad copy and visuals, can be personalized for target audiences to increase engagement and conversion rates.
- A/B Testing: Generative models can simulate and evaluate different marketing strategies and campaigns to identify the most effective approaches.

7. Transportation:

- Autonomous Vehicles: Generative models can simulate real-world driving scenarios to train and validate autonomous vehicle systems, improving their safety and reliability.

- Traffic Management: AI-generated traffic flow predictions and optimization strategies can help alleviate congestion and improve transportation efficiency in urban areas.

These are just a few examples of how generative AI is transforming industries by enabling innovative applications and solutions. As the technology continues to advance, we can expect to see even more impactful use cases emerge across various sectors.

CURRENT CHALLENGES FACED BY RETAILERS

Here's an overview of the retail industry with a focus on the current challenges faced by retailers:

Overview of the Retail Industry:

The retail industry encompasses businesses involved in the sale of goods and services to consumers. It is a vital component of the economy, driving employment, innovation, and consumer spending. Traditional brick-and-mortar retailers coexist with e-commerce platforms, and many businesses operate across both physical and online channels, adopting omnichannel strategies to meet consumer demands.

Current Challenges Faced by Retailers:

1. E-commerce Competition: The rise of e-commerce giants like Amazon has intensified competition for traditional retailers. Consumers increasingly prefer the convenience of online shopping, challenging brick-and-mortar stores to innovate and provide unique value propositions.

2. Changing Consumer Behavior: Consumer preferences and behaviors are evolving rapidly, driven by factors such as technological advancements, demographic shifts, and changing societal norms. Retailers must adapt to these changes to remain relevant and meet customer expectations.

3. Omnichannel Integration: Providing a seamless shopping experience across multiple channels, including physical stores, websites, mobile apps, and social media platforms, is essential for retailers. Achieving effective omnichannel integration requires investment in technology, logistics, and customer service.

4. Personalization and Customer Engagement: Consumers expect personalized shopping experiences tailored to their preferences and past interactions with the brand. Retailers must leverage data analytics and AI-driven technologies to deliver targeted marketing campaigns, product recommendations, and customer service experiences.

5. Supply Chain Disruptions: Global events such as the COVID-19 pandemic and geopolitical tensions have highlighted vulnerabilities in supply chains, leading to disruptions in manufacturing, distribution, and logistics. Retailers face challenges in managing inventory, fulfilling orders, and mitigating supply chain risks.

6. Rising Costs and Margins Pressure: Retailers contend with rising costs associated with rent, labor, utilities, and inventory management. Price competition and margin pressure further squeeze profitability, necessitating efficient operations and cost-saving measures.

7. Cybersecurity Threats: With the increasing digitization of retail operations and the collection of vast amounts of customer data, cybersecurity threats pose a significant risk to retailers. Data breaches, ransomware attacks, and payment fraud can result in financial losses, reputational damage, and legal liabilities.

8. Sustainability and Ethical Concerns: Consumers are increasingly conscious of environmental and social issues, demanding transparency and sustainability from retailers.

Meeting sustainability goals, ethical sourcing, and corporate social responsibility initiatives are critical for building brand trust and loyalty.

9. Regulatory Compliance: Retailers must comply with a myriad of regulations and industry standards related to consumer protection, data privacy, product safety, advertising practices, and labor laws. Non-compliance can result in fines, lawsuits, and reputational harm.

Addressing these challenges requires retailers to adopt a strategic approach, leveraging technology, data-driven insights, and innovation to enhance operational efficiency, customer experience, and competitive advantage in a rapidly evolving marketplace.

OPPORTUNITIES FOR AI IN RETAIL

The retail industry with a focus on the opportunities for AI:

1. Personalized Customer Experience: AI enables retailers to analyze vast amounts of customer data, including browsing history, purchase patterns, and demographic information, to deliver personalized shopping experiences. This includes personalized product recommendations, targeted marketing campaigns, and customized pricing strategies tailored to individual preferences.

2. Inventory Management and Demand Forecasting: AI-powered algorithms can optimize inventory levels, predict demand fluctuations, and automate replenishment processes, reducing stockouts, overstocking, and markdowns. Machine learning models analyze historical sales data, external factors (e.g., weather, seasonality), and market trends to generate accurate demand forecasts.

3. Visual Search and Product Discovery: AI-driven visual search technology allows consumers to search for products using images, enabling more intuitive and efficient product discovery. Retailers can enhance the search experience on their websites and mobile apps, improving engagement and conversion rates.

4. Chatbots and Virtual Assistants: AI-powered chatbots and virtual assistants provide round-the-clock customer support, answering inquiries, assisting with product recommendations, and facilitating purchases. Natural language processing (NLP)

algorithms enable chatbots to understand and respond to customer queries in real-time, enhancing the overall shopping experience.

5. Loss Prevention and Fraud Detection: AI algorithms analyze transaction data, customer behavior patterns, and historical fraud cases to identify suspicious activities and prevent fraudulent transactions in real-time. Retailers can leverage AI-driven fraud detection systems to minimize financial losses and protect against cyber threats.

6. Supply Chain Optimization: AI optimizes various aspects of the supply chain, including sourcing, transportation, warehousing, and distribution. Predictive analytics and machine learning algorithms improve supply chain visibility, mitigate risks, and optimize inventory routing and allocation, resulting in cost savings and operational efficiencies.

7. Dynamic Pricing and Revenue Management: AI enables retailers to implement dynamic pricing strategies based on factors such as demand elasticity, competitor pricing, and market conditions. Pricing algorithms continuously analyze data and adjust prices dynamically to maximize revenue, profitability, and competitiveness.

8. Customer Insights and Market Segmentation: AI-driven analytics platforms generate actionable insights from customer data, enabling retailers to identify trends, segment customer populations, and target specific market segments with tailored marketing strategies. Predictive analytics models forecast customer lifetime value, churn probability, and purchase intent, informing strategic decision-making and resource allocation.

9. Augmented Reality (AR) and Virtual Try-On: AR technology allows consumers to visualize products in their physical environment, such as trying on clothing or placing furniture in their homes virtually. Retailers can enhance the shopping experience, reduce returns, and increase conversion rates by

implementing AR-based virtual try-on solutions.

10. Voice Commerce: Voice-enabled virtual assistants, such as Amazon Alexa and Google Assistant, enable consumers to shop using voice commands, providing a hands-free and convenient shopping experience. Retailers can integrate voice commerce capabilities into their platforms, expanding their reach and accessibility to consumers.

By leveraging AI technologies, retailers can unlock new opportunities for growth, innovation, and competitive advantage in a rapidly evolving marketplace. Embracing AI-driven solutions empowers retailers to enhance customer experiences, optimize operations, and drive business outcomes in an increasingly digital and data-driven environment.

IMPORTANCE OF PERSONALIZATION IN RETAIL

Personalization is of paramount importance in the retail industry due to its significant impact on customer satisfaction, loyalty, and business success. Here's why personalization matters in retail:

1. Enhanced Customer Experience: Personalization allows retailers to tailor interactions, product recommendations, and marketing messages to individual customer preferences and behavior. By offering relevant and timely content, retailers can create a more engaging and enjoyable shopping experience, leading to higher customer satisfaction and loyalty.

2. Increased Customer Engagement: Personalized experiences capture consumers' attention and foster deeper engagement with the brand. By understanding customers' preferences, shopping habits, and purchase history, retailers can deliver targeted promotions, product suggestions, and loyalty rewards, encouraging repeat purchases and brand advocacy.

3. Improved Conversion Rates: Personalization helps retailers deliver the right product to the right customer at the right time, increasing the likelihood of conversion. By presenting relevant product recommendations and offers based on customers' interests and needs, retailers can drive impulse purchases and boost sales revenue.

4. Reduced Cart Abandonment: Personalized reminders and incentives can help reduce cart abandonment rates by prompting customers to complete their purchases. By sending targeted email reminders, push notifications, or personalized discounts, retailers can re-engage customers who have abandoned their shopping carts and encourage them to return to the website to complete their transactions.

5. Optimized Marketing ROI: Personalized marketing campaigns are more effective in driving customer engagement and conversion compared to generic mass marketing efforts. By targeting specific customer segments with personalized messages and offers, retailers can improve the return on investment (ROI) of their marketing spend and maximize revenue generation.

6. Customer Loyalty and Retention: Personalization fosters stronger emotional connections between customers and brands, leading to increased loyalty and repeat business. By demonstrating an understanding of customers' preferences and delivering personalized experiences consistently, retailers can build trust and loyalty over time, reducing churn and increasing customer lifetime value.

7. Competitive Differentiation: In a crowded marketplace, personalization serves as a key differentiator for retailers seeking to stand out from competitors. By offering personalized services, recommendations, and promotions that cater to individual customer needs, retailers can differentiate their brand and create a competitive advantage that drives customer acquisition and retention.

8. Data-Driven Insights: Personalization relies on data analytics and customer insights to understand individual preferences, behavior patterns, and purchase intent. By collecting and analyzing customer data effectively, retailers can gain valuable insights into consumer preferences, market trends, and

competitive dynamics, informing strategic decision-making and business planning.

In summary, personalization is essential for retailers to meet the evolving needs and expectations of today's consumers. By delivering tailored experiences, recommendations, and promotions, retailers can create meaningful connections with customers, drive engagement and loyalty, and ultimately, achieve business growth and success in a competitive marketplace.

NEURAL NETWORKS AND DEEP LEARNING

Let's delve into the fundamentals of generative models, starting with neural networks and deep learning:

Neural Networks:

Neural networks are computational models inspired by the structure and function of the human brain's interconnected neurons. They consist of layers of interconnected nodes (neurons) organized into an input layer, one or more hidden layers, and an output layer. Each neuron applies a mathematical transformation to its input and passes the result to the next layer.

- Input Layer: Neurons in the input layer receive the input data, which could be images, text, numerical values, etc.

- Hidden Layers: Hidden layers perform computations on the input data through a series of weighted connections and activation functions. Each neuron in a hidden layer receives inputs from the previous layer and produces an output based on its weighted sum of inputs and activation function.

- Output Layer: Neurons in the output layer produce the final output of the neural network, such as classification probabilities, regression values, or generated data samples.

Deep Learning:

Deep learning is a subfield of machine learning that focuses on training neural networks with multiple hidden layers to learn hierarchical representations of data. Deep learning models can automatically discover intricate patterns and features from raw input data, without the need for manual feature engineering.

Key concepts and techniques in deep learning include:

1. Backpropagation: A training algorithm that adjusts the weights of neural network connections to minimize the difference between predicted and actual outputs. Backpropagation computes the gradient of the loss function with respect to the network parameters, allowing for iterative optimization using gradient descent.

2. Activation Functions: Non-linear functions applied to the output of neurons in a neural network, enabling the model to learn complex mappings between inputs and outputs. Common activation functions include sigmoid, tanh, ReLU (Rectified Linear Unit), and softmax.

3. Convolutional Neural Networks (CNNs): Specialized neural networks designed for processing grid-like data, such as images. CNNs use convolutional layers to extract spatial hierarchies of features from input images, followed by pooling layers to reduce spatial dimensions and increase translation invariance.

4. Recurrent Neural Networks (RNNs): Neural networks capable of processing sequential data with temporal dependencies, such as text, audio, and time series. RNNs have recurrent connections that allow information to persist over time, enabling them to model sequential patterns and generate sequential outputs.

5. Generative Models: Neural networks trained to generate new data samples that resemble the training data distribution. Generative models, such as Generative Adversarial Networks (GANs) and Variational Autoencoders (VAEs), learn to map latent representations to output data samples, enabling them to generate realistic images, text, and other types of data.

Deep learning has revolutionized various fields, including computer vision, natural language processing, speech recognition, and reinforcement learning, by achieving state-of-the-art performance on a wide range of tasks. Generative models, in particular, leverage deep learning techniques to generate synthetic data with diverse applications in image synthesis, text generation, and creative content creation.

GENERATIVE ADVERSARIAL NETWORKS (GANS)

Generative Adversarial Networks (GANs) are a class of deep learning models introduced by Ian Goodfellow and his colleagues in 2014. GANs consist of two neural networks, the generator and the discriminator, which are trained simultaneously in a competitive manner.

Key Components:

1. Generator: The generator network takes random noise or latent vectors as input and generates synthetic data samples (e.g., images, text) that resemble real data. The goal of the generator is to produce outputs that are indistinguishable from real data samples.

2. Discriminator: The discriminator network evaluates the authenticity of data samples by distinguishing between real and generated samples. It is trained to classify whether a given input sample is real (from the training data) or fake (generated by the generator).

Training Process:

The training of GANs involves a minimax game between the generator and the discriminator:

1. Generator Training: Initially, the generator generates

synthetic samples from random noise. The discriminator then evaluates these samples and provides feedback on how well they resemble real data. The generator is trained to improve its ability to generate realistic samples by maximizing the probability that the discriminator incorrectly classifies its outputs as real.

2. Discriminator Training: Simultaneously, the discriminator is trained to distinguish between real and generated samples accurately. It learns to minimize the probability of misclassifying real samples as fake and vice versa.

3. Adversarial Training: The generator and discriminator are trained iteratively in a adversarial manner. As the generator improves its ability to generate realistic samples, the discriminator becomes better at distinguishing between real and fake samples. This adversarial process continues until an equilibrium is reached, where the generator produces high-quality samples that are difficult for the discriminator to differentiate from real data.

Applications of GANs:

1. Image Generation: GANs are widely used for generating realistic images, such as human faces, artwork, and landscapes. They can learn to generate images with diverse styles and characteristics, producing novel and visually appealing outputs.

2. Image-to-Image Translation: GANs can be used to translate images from one domain to another, such as converting black-and-white images to color, changing the season of a landscape, or altering the style of an artwork.

3. Super-Resolution: GANs can enhance the resolution and quality of low-resolution images, enabling applications in digital image upscaling and enhancement.

4. Data Augmentation: GANs can generate synthetic data samples to augment training datasets, improving the generalization and robustness of machine learning models.

5. Style Transfer: GANs can transfer artistic styles between images, allowing users to apply the visual characteristics of one image (e.g., painting style) to another image while preserving its content.

6. Drug Discovery: GANs are used in drug discovery and molecular design to generate novel molecular structures with desired properties, accelerating the drug development process.

Despite their remarkable capabilities, GANs pose challenges such as training instability, mode collapse, and evaluation metrics. Ongoing research focuses on addressing these challenges and extending the applicability of GANs to new domains and tasks.

VARIATIONAL AUTOENCODERS (VAES)

Variational Autoencoders (VAEs) are a type of generative model introduced by Kingma and Welling in 2013. VAEs are based on the framework of autoencoders, which are neural networks trained to reconstruct input data. VAEs extend the concept of traditional autoencoders to learn probabilistic representations of input data, enabling them to generate new data samples that resemble the training data distribution.

Key Components:

1. Encoder: The encoder network maps input data samples to latent space representations (latent vectors). It takes input data and outputs the parameters of a probability distribution (usually Gaussian) representing the latent variables.

2. Latent Space: Latent space represents the low-dimensional continuous space where data samples are encoded. Each point in the latent space corresponds to a potential input data sample.

3. Decoder (Generator): The decoder network takes latent vectors sampled from the latent space and reconstructs them into output data samples. It learns to generate outputs that resemble the original input data samples.

Training Process:

The training of VAEs involves maximizing the evidence lower bound (ELBO), which is an objective function that balances the reconstruction accuracy and the regularization of the latent space:

1. Reconstruction Loss: The reconstruction loss measures the difference between the input data samples and their reconstructions produced by the decoder. It encourages the decoder to generate outputs that closely resemble the original input data.

2. Regularization Term: The regularization term penalizes the divergence between the learned latent distribution and a prior distribution (usually a standard Gaussian). It encourages the encoder to produce latent representations that follow the prior distribution, promoting smoothness and continuity in the latent space.

3. Variational Inference: VAEs use variational inference to approximate the true posterior distribution of latent variables given input data. Instead of computing the exact posterior, which is often intractable, VAEs optimize a lower bound on the log-likelihood of the data.

Applications of VAEs:

1. Image Generation: VAEs can generate realistic images by sampling latent vectors from the learned distribution and decoding them into output images. They are used in applications such as image synthesis, image inpainting, and image editing.

2. Anomaly Detection: VAEs can learn to reconstruct normal patterns in data and identify anomalies as data samples that deviate significantly from the learned distribution. They are used for detecting anomalies in various domains, including fraud detection, cybersecurity, and medical diagnostics.

3. Data Imputation: VAEs can reconstruct missing or corrupted data by inpainting the missing parts based on the learned data distribution. They are used for data imputation tasks in healthcare, finance, and manufacturing.

4. Dimensionality Reduction: VAEs can learn low-dimensional representations of high-dimensional data, facilitating visualization, clustering, and classification tasks in machine learning.

5. Sequential Data Generation: VAEs can generate sequences of data samples, such as text, audio, or time series, by modeling the temporal dependencies in the data.

VAEs offer a powerful framework for learning probabilistic representations of data and generating new samples that capture the underlying structure of the data distribution. They have applications across various domains, including computer vision, natural language processing, and anomaly detection, and continue to be an active area of research in the field of deep learning and generative modeling.

FLOW-BASED MODELS

Flow-based models are a class of generative models that learn to model the probability distribution of data by transforming it through invertible transformations. These models are particularly useful for generating complex high-dimensional data, such as images, audio, and text, while preserving the tractability of the likelihood function and the ability to perform exact inference.

Key Concepts:

1. Invertible Transformations: Flow-based models apply a sequence of invertible transformations to the input data, such that both the forward transformation (from input to output) and the inverse transformation (from output to input) are computationally tractable. These transformations map the input data to a latent space where the probability distribution is more tractable.

2. Change of Variables: The likelihood of the observed data under the flow-based model is computed using the change of variables formula, which accounts for the transformation applied to the input data. The model learns the transformation parameters such that the likelihood of the observed data is maximized.

3. Coupling Layers: Coupling layers are a type of invertible transformation used in flow-based models. These layers split the input data into two parts, with one part transformed and the other part left unchanged. Coupling layers allow the model

to capture complex dependencies in the data while maintaining tractability.

4. Autoregressive Flows: Autoregressive flow-based models use autoregressive transformations to model the conditional dependencies between dimensions of the input data. These models sequentially transform each dimension of the input data based on the previously transformed dimensions, allowing them to capture complex dependencies in high-dimensional data.

Training Process:

Flow-based models are trained by maximizing the log-likelihood of the observed data using maximum likelihood estimation or variational inference techniques. The training process involves iteratively updating the parameters of the transformation functions to minimize the negative log-likelihood of the training data.

Applications of Flow-Based Models:

1. Image Generation: Flow-based models can generate realistic images by learning the probability distribution of pixel values in the training images. They are used for applications such as image synthesis, image editing, and style transfer.

2. Density Estimation: Flow-based models can estimate the probability density function of high-dimensional data, enabling tasks such as outlier detection, anomaly detection, and data visualization.

3. Data Compression: Flow-based models can learn compact representations of high-dimensional data by transforming it into a lower-dimensional latent space. These compact representations can be used for tasks such as data compression, dimensionality reduction, and feature extraction.

4. Inverse Problems: Flow-based models can be used to solve

inverse problems by learning the inverse transformation from the output space to the input space. This allows for tasks such as image super-resolution, image inpainting, and image denoising.

Flow-based models offer a flexible framework for generative modeling, capable of capturing complex dependencies in high-dimensional data while maintaining tractability and invertibility. They have applications across various domains, including computer vision, natural language processing, and signal processing, and continue to be an active area of research in the field of deep learning and generative modeling.

PRODUCT IMAGE GENERATION

Product image generation is a powerful application of generative AI in the retail industry. Here's how it works and its benefits:

Product Image Generation:

Generative AI models, particularly Generative Adversarial Networks (GANs) and Variational Autoencoders (VAEs), can be trained on large datasets of product images to generate new, realistic-looking images of products that may not exist in reality. These models learn the underlying patterns and features of the training images and use them to synthesize novel images that are visually indistinguishable from real product photographs.

How it Works:

1. Training Data: Generative models are trained on a diverse dataset of product images from various categories such as clothing, accessories, electronics, furniture, and more. The dataset should encompass different styles, colors, shapes, and perspectives to enable the model to learn a broad range of visual characteristics.

2. Model Training: The generative model, typically a GAN or VAE, is trained on the dataset of product images using techniques such as adversarial training or variational inference. During training, the model learns to capture the underlying distribution of the training images and generate new images that closely resemble real products.

3. Image Generation: Once trained, the generative model can generate new product images by sampling from the learned latent space or by conditioning the generation process on specific attributes or styles. The generated images can exhibit variations in color, texture, shape, and other visual attributes, allowing for diverse and creative outputs.

4. Quality Evaluation: The quality of the generated images is assessed based on their visual realism, coherence, and fidelity to the training data distribution. Evaluation metrics and human judgment are used to validate the generated images and ensure their suitability for use in retail applications.

Benefits:

1. Cost-Effective Content Creation: Product image generation using generative AI eliminates the need for expensive and time-consuming photoshoots for every product in a retailer's inventory. It enables retailers to create high-quality product images at scale, reducing production costs and turnaround times.

2. Product Variation and Customization: Generative AI allows retailers to generate images of products in different variations, styles, colors, and configurations without physically manufacturing each variant. This enables retailers to showcase a broader range of product options and cater to diverse customer preferences.

3. Rapid Prototyping and Design Iteration: Product image generation facilitates rapid prototyping and design iteration by quickly visualizing new product concepts and designs. Retailers can generate virtual prototypes, experiment with different aesthetics, and gather feedback from stakeholders before committing to physical production.

4. Seasonal and Trend-Based Merchandising: Generative AI enables retailers to generate product images aligned with

seasonal themes, holidays, or current fashion trends. They can create seasonal collections, promotional campaigns, and trend-driven assortments to capitalize on market trends and consumer preferences.

5. Enhanced Visual Merchandising: Product image generation enhances visual merchandising efforts by providing retailers with a diverse set of visually appealing images for online catalogs, digital signage, social media marketing, and other promotional channels. It improves the overall presentation of products and enhances the shopping experience for customers.

Overall, product image generation powered by generative AI offers retailers a scalable, cost-effective, and creative solution for content creation, merchandising, and design innovation in the competitive retail landscape. It enables retailers to differentiate their brand, engage customers, and drive sales through compelling visual content that showcases their product offerings effectively.

VIRTUAL TRY-ON AND AUGMENTED REALITY

Virtual try-on and augmented reality (AR) are innovative applications of generative AI in the retail industry, revolutionizing the way customers shop for clothing, accessories, and other fashion items. Here's how these technologies work and their benefits:

Virtual Try-On:

Virtual try-on allows customers to visualize how clothing, accessories, and cosmetics will look on them without physically trying them on. Generative AI models, particularly computer vision algorithms, analyze images or live video feeds of customers and overlay virtual representations of products onto their bodies in real-time.

How it Works:

1. Body Detection and Tracking: Computer vision algorithms detect and track the customer's body and key landmarks, such as joints and contours, in the input images or video frames.

2. Virtual Product Overlay: Generative AI models overlay virtual representations of products, such as clothing items or accessories, onto the customer's body based on their size, shape, and pose. The virtual products are rendered to match the customer's body proportions and movement.

3. Real-Time Visualization: The virtual try-on system provides

customers with a real-time visualization of how the products will look on them from different angles and perspectives. Customers can interact with the virtual products, explore different styles, colors, and sizes, and make informed purchase decisions.

Benefits:

1. Enhanced Shopping Experience: Virtual try-on enhances the shopping experience by providing customers with a realistic and immersive way to visualize products before making a purchase. It reduces uncertainty and hesitation by allowing customers to see how products will fit and look on them.

2. Increased Confidence and Satisfaction: Virtual try-on builds confidence and satisfaction among customers by enabling them to explore and experiment with different styles and looks in a risk-free virtual environment. It empowers customers to make personalized choices that align with their preferences and tastes.

3. Reduced Returns and Exchanges: Virtual try-on helps reduce returns and exchanges by enabling customers to make more informed purchasing decisions. Customers can accurately assess how products will fit and look on them, leading to fewer instances of dissatisfaction or mismatched expectations.

4. Personalized Recommendations: Virtual try-on data can be used to generate personalized product recommendations based on customers' preferences, body measurements, and past interactions. Retailers can leverage this data to offer tailored suggestions and upsell complementary products.

AUGMENTED REALITY (AR):

Augmented reality (AR) enhances the real-world environment with digital overlays, enabling customers to visualize products in their physical surroundings. AR applications in retail use generative AI to place virtual representations of products, such as furniture, home decor, or cosmetics, within the customer's space.

How it Works:

1. Environment Mapping: AR systems use sensors, cameras, and depth-sensing technologies to map and understand the customer's physical environment, including walls, floors, and objects.

2. Virtual Product Placement: Generative AI models overlay virtual representations of products onto the customer's environment, aligning them with the physical space and scale. Customers can interact with the virtual products, move them around, and see how they fit within their space.

3. Real-Time Visualization: AR applications provide customers with a real-time visualization of how products will look and fit within their home or surroundings. Customers can explore different styles, colors, and configurations and make informed purchase decisions.

Benefits:

1. Visualize Products in Context: AR enables customers to visualize products in their real-world context, helping them assess how products will look, fit, and complement their existing environment. It enhances the shopping experience by providing a more immersive and interactive way to explore products.

2. Reduce Purchase Uncertainty: AR reduces purchase uncertainty by allowing customers to see how products will look in their space before making a purchase. It minimizes the risk of buyer's remorse and increases confidence in purchasing decisions.

3. Customization and Personalization: AR applications can offer customization options, allowing customers to personalize products, such as furniture or home decor, to suit their preferences and style. Customers can experiment with different configurations, colors, and finishes to create unique and personalized solutions.

4. Streamline Decision-Making: AR streamlines the decision-making process by providing customers with a visual representation of products in their environment. It helps customers compare options, assess compatibility, and make informed choices without the need for physical samples or showroom visits.

Overall, virtual try-on and augmented reality powered by generative AI offer retailers innovative ways to engage customers, enhance the shopping experience, and drive sales in an increasingly digital and competitive retail landscape. These technologies leverage the capabilities of generative AI to deliver personalized, immersive, and interactive experiences that cater to the evolving preferences and expectations of modern consumers.

CONTENT CREATION AND MARKETING

Generative AI has transformative applications in content creation and marketing for the retail industry, enabling retailers to produce personalized, engaging, and visually appealing content at scale. Here's how generative AI is revolutionizing content creation and marketing in retail:

Content Creation:

1. Product Descriptions and Copywriting: Generative AI can generate compelling product descriptions, marketing copy, and promotional content based on product attributes, customer preferences, and brand guidelines. It automates the process of content creation, saving time and resources while ensuring consistency and quality.

2. Social Media Posts and Captions: Generative AI can create social media posts, captions, and hashtags tailored to specific platforms and target audiences. It generates engaging content that resonates with customers, drives interaction, and increases brand visibility across social media channels.

3. Email Marketing Campaigns: Generative AI assists retailers in creating personalized email marketing campaigns by generating subject lines, body content, and call-to-action messages optimized for individual recipients. It enhances email engagement and conversion rates by delivering relevant and compelling content to subscribers.

4. Blog Posts and Articles: Generative AI can produce blog posts, articles, and editorial content on topics relevant to the retail industry, such as fashion trends, styling tips, product reviews, and industry insights. It generates informative and engaging content that attracts readers, enhances brand authority, and drives website traffic.

Marketing:

1. Personalized Product Recommendations: Generative AI analyzes customer data, purchase history, and browsing behavior to generate personalized product recommendations across various touchpoints, including websites, mobile apps, email campaigns, and social media ads. It enhances the relevance of product suggestions and increases conversion rates by delivering tailored recommendations to individual customers.

2. Dynamic Pricing and Promotions: Generative AI optimizes pricing and promotional strategies by analyzing market dynamics, competitor pricing, demand forecasts, and customer segmentation. It generates dynamic pricing models and promotional offers that maximize revenue, profitability, and customer satisfaction while responding to changes in market conditions and consumer preferences.

3. Visual Content Generation: Generative AI creates visual content, such as images, graphics, videos, and animations, for marketing campaigns, advertisements, and social media posts. It generates visually appealing and brand-consistent assets that capture customers' attention, communicate key messages, and drive engagement across digital channels.

4. A/B Testing and Optimization: Generative AI facilitates A/B testing and optimization of marketing campaigns by generating variations of ad creatives, landing pages, and messaging. It automates the experimentation process, identifies

high-performing variants, and iteratively improves campaign performance based on real-time feedback and analytics.

5. Influencer Marketing: Generative AI analyzes influencer profiles, audience demographics, and engagement metrics to identify suitable influencers for collaboration. It generates personalized outreach messages, sponsorship proposals, and content briefs tailored to individual influencers, maximizing the effectiveness of influencer marketing campaigns.

6. Customer Segmentation and Targeting: Generative AI segments customers into distinct groups based on demographic, behavioral, and psychographic characteristics. It generates targeted marketing campaigns and communication strategies tailored to each segment's preferences, interests, and purchasing behavior, enhancing the relevance and effectiveness of marketing efforts.

Generative AI empowers retailers to create personalized, data-driven, and impactful content and marketing campaigns that resonate with customers, drive engagement, and ultimately, increase sales and brand loyalty. By leveraging the capabilities of generative AI, retailers can streamline content creation workflows, optimize marketing strategies, and deliver exceptional customer experiences in an increasingly competitive and dynamic retail landscape.

DEMAND FORECASTING AND INVENTORY MANAGEMENT

Generative AI plays a crucial role in demand forecasting and inventory management for the retail industry, enabling retailers to optimize inventory levels, minimize stockouts, reduce excess inventory, and improve supply chain efficiency. Here's how generative AI is transforming demand forecasting and inventory management in retail:

Demand Forecasting:

1. Predictive Analytics: Generative AI models analyze historical sales data, customer behavior patterns, market trends, and external factors (e.g., seasonality, promotions, economic indicators) to generate accurate demand forecasts for individual products, categories, or regions. It leverages machine learning algorithms to identify patterns, correlations, and seasonality in the data and predict future demand with high accuracy.

2. Dynamic Demand Modeling: Generative AI enables retailers to model dynamic demand patterns and adapt forecasts in real-time based on changing market conditions, consumer preferences, and external events (e.g., holidays, weather events, supply chain disruptions). It provides retailers with actionable

insights and recommendations for adjusting inventory levels, pricing strategies, and promotional activities to meet fluctuating demand effectively.

3. Demand Sensing: Generative AI enhances demand sensing capabilities by integrating real-time data streams, such as point-of-sale transactions, social media mentions, online search trends, and weather forecasts, into demand forecasting models. It enables retailers to capture short-term demand signals, detect demand anomalies, and respond quickly to emerging trends or demand fluctuations in the market.

4. Scenario Planning: Generative AI facilitates scenario planning and sensitivity analysis by simulating different scenarios, what-if scenarios, and hypothetical demand scenarios to evaluate the impact of various factors on demand forecasts and inventory requirements. It helps retailers anticipate risks, mitigate uncertainties, and develop contingency plans to adapt to changing market dynamics proactively.

Inventory Management:

1. Optimized Replenishment: Generative AI optimizes inventory replenishment processes by aligning inventory levels with forecasted demand, lead times, service level targets, and cost constraints. It determines optimal reorder points, reorder quantities, and safety stock levels to minimize stockouts, backorders, and excess inventory while maximizing inventory turnover and fill rates.

2. Dynamic Inventory Allocation: Generative AI dynamically allocates inventory across channels, locations, and distribution centers based on demand forecasts, inventory levels, shipping constraints, and customer preferences. It ensures that products are available where and when they are needed most, optimizing the allocation of scarce resources and minimizing stock imbalances.

3. Seasonal Demand Management: Generative AI helps retailers manage seasonal demand patterns by predicting seasonal trends, adjusting inventory levels accordingly, and optimizing seasonal inventory allocation and replenishment strategies. It enables retailers to capitalize on seasonal opportunities, minimize excess inventory carryover, and reduce markdowns at the end of the season.

4. Supplier Collaboration: Generative AI facilitates collaboration with suppliers and vendors by sharing demand forecasts, inventory data, and supply chain insights in real-time. It enables retailers to work closely with suppliers to align production schedules, manage lead times, and optimize order fulfillment processes, ensuring timely delivery of products and reducing supply chain disruptions.

5. Supply Chain Optimization: Generative AI optimizes various aspects of the supply chain, including sourcing, transportation, warehousing, and distribution, to improve inventory management and reduce costs. It leverages predictive analytics and machine learning algorithms to optimize inventory routing, minimize stockouts, and streamline order fulfillment processes, resulting in improved supply chain efficiency and resilience.

By harnessing the power of generative AI for demand forecasting and inventory management, retailers can enhance their ability to anticipate customer demand, optimize inventory levels, and deliver superior customer experiences while reducing costs and improving operational efficiency across the supply chain.

PERSONALIZED RECOMMENDATIONS

Enhancing customer experience through personalized recommendations is a powerful application of generative AI in retail. By leveraging customer data and machine learning algorithms, retailers can deliver tailored product suggestions that resonate with individual preferences, interests, and buying behavior. Here's how generative AI enhances personalized recommendations to enrich the customer experience:

1. Data-driven Insights: Generative AI analyzes vast amounts of customer data, including purchase history, browsing behavior, demographic information, and contextual data, to gain insights into individual preferences, trends, and patterns. By understanding customer preferences and intent, retailers can generate personalized recommendations that align with each customer's unique needs and interests.

2. Recommendation Engines: Generative AI powers recommendation engines that utilize collaborative filtering, content-based filtering, and hybrid approaches to generate personalized product recommendations. These recommendation algorithms analyze historical interactions and similarities between customers and products to identify relevant items and suggest them to customers in real-time across various touchpoints, such as websites, mobile apps, email campaigns, and social media ads.

3. Dynamic Personalization: Generative AI enables dynamic

personalization of recommendations based on contextual factors, such as time of day, location, device type, and browsing context. Retailers can tailor recommendations to match customers' current needs, preferences, and situational contexts, providing relevant and timely suggestions that enhance the shopping experience and drive engagement.

4. Multimodal Recommendations: Generative AI incorporates multimodal data sources, such as images, text, and user-generated content, to generate diverse and engaging product recommendations. Retailers can leverage visual search, natural language processing (NLP), and sentiment analysis techniques to understand customer preferences expressed through images, reviews, and social media interactions, and generate recommendations that resonate with visual and textual cues.

5. Serendipity and Discovery: Generative AI introduces serendipity and discovery into the recommendation process by surfacing unexpected or complementary products that customers may not have considered but are likely to be interested in based on their preferences and purchase history. By introducing variety and novelty into the recommendations, retailers can encourage exploration, discovery, and impulse purchases, enriching the overall shopping experience.

6. Continual Learning and Adaptation: Generative AI models continuously learn from customer interactions, feedback, and evolving preferences to refine and adapt recommendations over time. By incorporating feedback loops and reinforcement learning techniques, retailers can optimize recommendation algorithms to deliver increasingly relevant and personalized suggestions that reflect changing customer preferences and market trends.

7. Ethical and Transparent Recommendations: Generative AI prioritizes ethical considerations and transparency in recommendation systems by ensuring fairness, diversity,

and accountability in the recommendation process. Retailers adopt responsible AI practices, such as avoiding bias in recommendations, respecting user privacy and consent, and providing transparency into how recommendations are generated and personalized, to build trust and confidence among customers.

By harnessing the capabilities of generative AI for personalized recommendations, retailers can create differentiated, engaging, and memorable shopping experiences that cater to the individual preferences and needs of each customer. By delivering relevant and timely product suggestions, retailers can drive customer engagement, loyalty, and satisfaction, ultimately leading to increased sales and business growth.

CHATBOTS AND VIRTUAL ASSISTANTS

Generative AI enhances customer experience through the deployment of chatbots and virtual assistants, providing personalized, efficient, and interactive support across various touchpoints. Here's how generative AI improves customer experience through chatbots and virtual assistants:

1. 24/7 Availability: Generative AI-powered chatbots and virtual assistants are available 24/7, enabling customers to access support and assistance at any time, regardless of business hours or time zones. This round-the-clock availability ensures that customers receive timely responses and assistance whenever they need it, enhancing convenience and satisfaction.

2. Instant Responses: Chatbots and virtual assistants powered by generative AI deliver instant responses to customer inquiries, questions, and requests. By leveraging natural language processing (NLP) and machine learning algorithms, these AI-powered assistants understand customer queries and provide accurate, contextually relevant answers in real-time, reducing wait times and improving responsiveness.

3. Personalized Interactions: Generative AI enables chatbots and virtual assistants to engage in personalized interactions with customers based on their preferences, history, and context. These AI-powered assistants can tailor responses, recommendations, and assistance to each customer's unique needs, providing a customized and relevant experience that

fosters engagement and loyalty.

4. Multichannel Support: Chatbots and virtual assistants equipped with generative AI capabilities offer multichannel support across various communication channels, including websites, mobile apps, messaging platforms, and voice interfaces. Customers can interact with AI-powered assistants seamlessly across different touchpoints, choosing the channel that best suits their preferences and needs.

5. Natural Language Understanding: Generative AI enables chatbots and virtual assistants to understand and interpret natural language queries, colloquial language, and variations in language patterns. By employing advanced NLP techniques, these AI-powered assistants can comprehend complex queries, resolve ambiguities, and engage in human-like conversations that mimic the nuances of human communication.

6. Task Automation: Chatbots and virtual assistants streamline customer service processes by automating repetitive tasks, such as FAQs, order tracking, appointment scheduling, and basic troubleshooting. Generative AI-powered assistants can handle routine inquiries and transactions autonomously, freeing up human agents to focus on more complex or specialized customer interactions, enhancing efficiency and productivity.

7. Continuous Learning and Improvement: Generative AI models used in chatbots and virtual assistants continually learn from customer interactions, feedback, and data to improve their performance and accuracy over time. By leveraging machine learning algorithms and reinforcement learning techniques, these AI-powered assistants adapt to evolving customer needs, preferences, and behaviors, delivering increasingly relevant and effective assistance.

8. Seamless Handoff to Human Agents: Chatbots and virtual assistants seamlessly hand off conversations to human agents when complex issues arise or when customers require

personalized assistance beyond the capabilities of AI. This smooth transition ensures that customers receive the support and attention they need while maintaining continuity and context throughout the interaction.

By leveraging generative AI for chatbots and virtual assistants, retailers can deliver personalized, efficient, and responsive customer support that enhances satisfaction, fosters engagement, and drives loyalty. These AI-powered assistants play a pivotal role in providing seamless and frictionless customer experiences across all stages of the customer journey, ultimately contributing to increased customer retention and business success.

CUSTOMIZED SHOPPING EXPERIENCES

Generative AI empowers retailers to create customized shopping experiences that cater to the unique preferences, tastes, and needs of individual customers. By leveraging customer data, machine learning algorithms, and generative models, retailers can personalize every aspect of the shopping journey, from product discovery to purchase, delivery, and post-purchase engagement. Here's how generative AI enhances customer experience through customized shopping experiences:

1. Personalized Product Recommendations: Generative AI analyzes customer data, including purchase history, browsing behavior, and demographic information, to generate personalized product recommendations tailored to each customer's preferences and interests. By leveraging collaborative filtering, content-based filtering, and hybrid recommendation algorithms, retailers can surface relevant products that resonate with individual customers, driving engagement and increasing conversion rates.

2. Interactive Product Visualization: Generative AI enables interactive product visualization tools, such as virtual try-on, augmented reality (AR), and 3D product configurators, that allow customers to visualize and customize products in real-time. By leveraging computer vision, 3D modeling,

and rendering techniques, retailers can create immersive and interactive shopping experiences that empower customers to explore, customize, and personalize products according to their preferences and style.

3. Customized Product Design: Generative AI facilitates customized product design and personalization by enabling customers to co-create and customize products according to their preferences, specifications, and requirements. By offering customization options, such as monogramming, engraving, and color selection, retailers can empower customers to create unique and one-of-a-kind products that reflect their individuality and style.

4. Tailored Pricing and Promotions: Generative AI optimizes pricing and promotional strategies by segmenting customers into distinct groups based on their purchasing behavior, preferences, and lifecycle stage. By offering personalized discounts, coupons, and incentives, retailers can reward loyal customers, incentivize repeat purchases, and encourage upselling and cross-selling, enhancing customer loyalty and lifetime value.

5. Contextual Content and Messaging: Generative AI generates contextual content and messaging that resonate with individual customers based on their preferences, behavior, and context. By leveraging natural language processing (NLP) and sentiment analysis, retailers can tailor product descriptions, marketing copy, and communication channels to match each customer's interests, preferences, and communication preferences, fostering engagement and loyalty.

6. Predictive Customer Service: Generative AI predicts customer service needs and proactively addresses issues before they arise by analyzing historical data, customer interactions, and predictive analytics. By anticipating customer needs, retailers can provide proactive support, personalized recommendations,

and timely assistance that enhances satisfaction and loyalty while reducing customer effort and frustration.

7. Post-Purchase Engagement: Generative AI enhances post-purchase engagement by delivering personalized follow-up communications, product recommendations, and loyalty rewards based on each customer's purchase history and behavior. By leveraging customer segmentation, lifecycle analysis, and predictive modeling, retailers can nurture customer relationships, encourage repeat purchases, and foster brand advocacy, driving long-term loyalty and advocacy.

By harnessing the capabilities of generative AI for customized shopping experiences, retailers can create differentiated and memorable experiences that delight customers, drive engagement, and foster long-term loyalty and advocacy. These personalized experiences not only enhance customer satisfaction and loyalty but also drive business growth and competitive advantage in the dynamic and evolving retail landscape.

DYNAMIC PRICING STRATEGIES

Dynamic pricing strategies powered by generative AI enhance customer experience by offering personalized and optimized pricing tailored to individual preferences, behavior, and market dynamics. Here's how generative AI enhances customer experience through dynamic pricing strategies:

1. Personalized Pricing: Generative AI analyzes customer data, including purchase history, browsing behavior, demographics, and preferences, to generate personalized pricing offers tailored to each customer's profile and purchasing patterns. By leveraging machine learning algorithms, retailers can segment customers into distinct groups and offer customized discounts, coupons, and promotions that resonate with individual preferences, driving engagement and increasing conversion rates.

2. Real-Time Pricing Adjustments: Generative AI enables retailers to adjust prices dynamically in real-time based on changes in demand, supply, competition, and other market factors. By monitoring market conditions, competitor pricing, and customer sentiment, retailers can optimize prices to maximize revenue, profitability, and customer satisfaction while remaining competitive and responsive to market dynamics.

3. Demand-Based Pricing: Generative AI models forecast demand and predict price elasticity for different products,

categories, and customer segments, enabling retailers to implement demand-based pricing strategies. By adjusting prices based on demand fluctuations, seasonality, and other factors, retailers can optimize revenue, reduce stockouts, and minimize excess inventory while maintaining competitive pricing and satisfying customer demand.

4. Personalized Discounts and Incentives: Generative AI generates personalized discounts, coupons, and incentives tailored to each customer's preferences, behavior, and purchase history. By offering targeted promotions and incentives, retailers can reward loyal customers, incentivize repeat purchases, and encourage upselling and cross-selling, enhancing customer loyalty and lifetime value while driving incremental sales and revenue.

5. Dynamic Pricing Algorithms: Generative AI develops dynamic pricing algorithms that optimize prices based on predictive analytics, machine learning models, and optimization techniques. By considering factors such as demand forecasts, inventory levels, competitor pricing, and customer segmentation, retailers can dynamically adjust prices to maximize revenue, margin, and customer satisfaction while balancing supply and demand dynamics in real-time.

6. Transparent and Fair Pricing: Generative AI ensures transparency and fairness in dynamic pricing strategies by providing clear explanations and justifications for price changes. By communicating pricing policies, algorithms, and factors influencing pricing decisions, retailers build trust and confidence among customers, reducing perceived price unfairness and increasing acceptance of dynamic pricing practices.

7. Price Discrimination Mitigation: Generative AI mitigates price discrimination risks by implementing pricing strategies that are fair, transparent, and compliant with regulatory requirements.

By avoiding discriminatory pricing practices based on sensitive attributes such as race, gender, or socioeconomic status, retailers uphold ethical standards and protect customer trust and loyalty, fostering positive relationships and long-term brand loyalty.

By leveraging the capabilities of generative AI for dynamic pricing strategies, retailers can create personalized and optimized pricing experiences that enhance customer satisfaction, loyalty, and engagement while maximizing revenue, profitability, and competitive advantage in the dynamic and competitive retail landscape. These personalized pricing strategies not only drive short-term sales but also build long-term customer relationships and brand loyalty, driving sustainable business growth and success.

PREDICTIVE MAINTENANCE

Leveraging generative AI for predictive maintenance in supply chain optimization involves using machine learning models to predict when equipment or machinery is likely to fail, allowing proactive maintenance to be performed before breakdowns occur. Here's how generative AI can be applied to predictive maintenance in the supply chain:

1. Data Collection and Monitoring: Generative AI collects and monitors data from various sources, such as sensors, IoT devices, and historical maintenance records, to track the health and performance of equipment and machinery in the supply chain. Data may include operating conditions, temperature, vibration, pressure, and other indicators of equipment health.

2. Feature Extraction and Engineering: Generative AI extracts relevant features from the collected data and engineers new features to represent the underlying patterns and relationships indicative of equipment failure. This may involve time-series analysis, signal processing, and feature transformation techniques to extract meaningful information from raw sensor data.

3. Model Training: Generative AI trains machine learning models, such as recurrent neural networks (RNNs), long short-term memory (LSTM) networks, or convolutional neural networks (CNNs), on historical data to learn patterns of equipment behavior leading to failure. These models are trained

to predict future equipment failures based on input features such as sensor readings, maintenance logs, and environmental conditions.

4. Anomaly Detection: Generative AI detects anomalies in equipment behavior by comparing real-time sensor data to the patterns learned during model training. When deviations from normal operating conditions are detected, the AI system alerts maintenance personnel to investigate potential issues and take preventive action before equipment failure occurs.

5. Probabilistic Forecasting: Generative AI generates probabilistic forecasts of equipment failure probabilities based on predictive models and historical data. These forecasts provide insights into the likelihood and timing of future maintenance events, allowing supply chain managers to prioritize maintenance tasks and allocate resources efficiently.

6. Optimized Maintenance Scheduling: Generative AI optimizes maintenance scheduling by considering factors such as equipment criticality, maintenance costs, operational impact, and supply chain constraints. By predicting maintenance needs in advance, supply chain managers can plan and schedule maintenance activities during periods of low demand or downtime, minimizing disruption to operations and maximizing equipment uptime.

7. Continuous Learning and Improvement: Generative AI continuously learns from new data and feedback to improve the accuracy and reliability of predictive maintenance models. By incorporating real-time data updates, model retraining, and performance monitoring, the AI system adapts to changing equipment conditions and evolving maintenance requirements, ensuring optimal performance over time.

By leveraging generative AI for predictive maintenance in the supply chain, organizations can reduce unplanned downtime, minimize maintenance costs, and optimize equipment performance and reliability. Proactive maintenance practices enabled by generative AI not only improve operational efficiency and asset utilization but also enhance overall supply chain resilience and competitiveness in the global marketplace.

ROUTE OPTIMIZATION

Generative AI can significantly enhance route optimization in supply chain management by leveraging machine learning algorithms to analyze complex data sets, identify patterns, and generate optimal routes for transportation and logistics operations. Here's how generative AI can be applied to route optimization in the supply chain:

1. Data Collection and Integration: Generative AI collects and integrates data from various sources, including historical transportation data, real-time traffic information, weather forecasts, customer locations, and delivery constraints. This data is used to build a comprehensive understanding of the supply chain network, including the locations of warehouses, distribution centers, suppliers, and customers.

2. Network Modeling: Generative AI models the supply chain network as a graph, with nodes representing locations (e.g., warehouses, distribution centers, customers) and edges representing transportation links (e.g., roads, railways, shipping lanes). The AI system analyzes the network topology, distances between nodes, transportation capacities, and other constraints to formulate the optimization problem.

3. Optimization Objectives: Generative AI defines optimization objectives based on specific supply chain goals, such as minimizing transportation costs, reducing delivery times, maximizing vehicle utilization, or minimizing carbon

emissions. These objectives are translated into mathematical optimization models that the AI system aims to solve efficiently.

4. Algorithm Selection: Generative AI employs a variety of optimization algorithms and techniques to solve the route optimization problem effectively. These may include heuristic algorithms (e.g., genetic algorithms, simulated annealing), metaheuristic algorithms (e.g., ant colony optimization, particle swarm optimization), or exact optimization methods (e.g., mixed-integer linear programming, dynamic programming).

5. Constraints Management: Generative AI manages various constraints and considerations in route optimization, including vehicle capacities, time windows for deliveries, vehicle availability, driver schedules, traffic conditions, and regulatory requirements (e.g., driving hours, weight restrictions). The AI system ensures that optimized routes adhere to these constraints while achieving the desired optimization objectives.

6. Real-Time Adaptation: Generative AI enables real-time adaptation of route plans based on changing conditions, such as traffic congestion, accidents, weather disruptions, or unexpected events. The AI system continuously monitors the supply chain environment and updates route plans dynamically to minimize disruptions and optimize delivery performance.

7. Scenario Analysis and Sensitivity Testing: Generative AI conducts scenario analysis and sensitivity testing to evaluate the robustness and resilience of route plans under different scenarios and conditions. By simulating various what-if scenarios, such as changes in demand patterns, fuel prices, or capacity constraints, the AI system identifies potential risks and opportunities and adjusts route plans accordingly.

8. Continuous Learning and Improvement: Generative AI continuously learns from new data, feedback, and optimization results to improve route optimization algorithms and models over time. By incorporating historical performance data,

customer feedback, and operational insights, the AI system iteratively refines its optimization strategies and adapts to evolving supply chain dynamics.

By leveraging generative AI for route optimization in the supply chain, organizations can improve efficiency, reduce costs, enhance customer satisfaction, and increase competitiveness in the marketplace. Optimized routes enable faster deliveries, lower transportation costs, reduced environmental impact, and improved overall supply chain performance, driving value and enabling organizations to meet the evolving demands of modern commerce.

SUPPLIER MANAGEMENT

Generative AI can significantly enhance supplier management in supply chain optimization by leveraging machine learning algorithms to analyze supplier data, identify patterns, and optimize supplier selection, performance, and relationships. Here's how generative AI can be applied to supplier management in the supply chain:

1. Supplier Data Integration: Generative AI integrates and consolidates supplier data from various sources, including supplier databases, transaction records, performance metrics, contracts, and compliance documents. This data provides a comprehensive view of supplier relationships, capabilities, and performance metrics, enabling informed decision-making in supplier management.

2. Supplier Segmentation: Generative AI segments suppliers into distinct categories based on various criteria, such as product categories, geographical locations, performance metrics, risk profiles, and strategic importance. By clustering suppliers into meaningful segments, the AI system can prioritize resources and tailor management strategies to meet the specific needs and requirements of each supplier segment.

3. Supplier Performance Monitoring: Generative AI monitors supplier performance using key performance indicators (KPIs) and performance metrics, such as on-time delivery, quality, lead times, responsiveness, and cost-effectiveness. By analyzing

historical performance data and real-time updates, the AI system identifies trends, patterns, and deviations in supplier performance and alerts supply chain managers to potential issues or opportunities for improvement.

4. Predictive Supplier Analytics: Generative AI employs predictive analytics to forecast supplier performance and identify potential risks or opportunities in supplier relationships. By analyzing historical data, market trends, and external factors, the AI system predicts future supplier behavior, such as delivery delays, quality issues, or capacity constraints, allowing supply chain managers to proactively mitigate risks and optimize supplier relationships.

5. Supplier Relationship Management (SRM): Generative AI supports supplier relationship management by fostering collaboration, transparency, and trust between buyers and suppliers. The AI system facilitates communication, feedback exchange, and performance reviews between supply chain partners, enabling constructive dialogue and continuous improvement in supplier relationships.

6. Supplier Risk Management: Generative AI assesses supplier risk using advanced risk modeling techniques, such as risk scoring, scenario analysis, and risk mapping. By evaluating factors such as financial stability, geopolitical risks, regulatory compliance, and supply chain disruptions, the AI system identifies potential risks in the supplier base and develops mitigation strategies to minimize supply chain disruptions and vulnerabilities.

7. Supplier Selection and Sourcing Optimization: Generative AI optimizes supplier selection and sourcing decisions by evaluating supplier capabilities, performance, and cost-effectiveness against specific sourcing criteria and business objectives. By employing optimization algorithms and decision support systems, the AI system identifies the most suitable

suppliers for each sourcing requirement, balancing factors such as quality, price, lead times, and strategic alignment.

8. Continuous Improvement and Innovation: Generative AI fosters continuous improvement and innovation in supplier management by providing insights, recommendations, and feedback loops for ongoing performance improvement. By leveraging machine learning algorithms and natural language processing (NLP) techniques, the AI system identifies opportunities for innovation, cost reduction, and process optimization in supplier relationships, driving value and competitiveness in the supply chain.

By leveraging generative AI for supplier management in the supply chain, organizations can optimize supplier relationships, mitigate risks, improve performance, and drive innovation, ultimately enhancing supply chain efficiency, resilience, and competitiveness in the global marketplace. Generative AI enables organizations to harness the power of data-driven insights and predictive analytics to make informed decisions and achieve strategic objectives in supplier management and supply chain optimization.

QUALITY CONTROL

Generative AI can significantly enhance quality control in supply chain optimization by leveraging machine learning algorithms to analyze production data, identify defects, and optimize quality assurance processes. Here's how generative AI can be applied to quality control in the supply chain:

1. Data Collection and Integration: Generative AI collects and integrates data from various sources, including production equipment, sensors, quality inspection records, and customer feedback. This data provides insights into production processes, product quality, and potential defects, enabling proactive quality management in the supply chain.

2. Defect Detection and Classification: Generative AI employs computer vision algorithms to detect and classify defects in manufactured products using image recognition and pattern recognition techniques. By analyzing images and visual data from production lines, the AI system identifies anomalies, deviations, and defects in product quality, enabling timely intervention and corrective action.

3. Predictive Quality Analytics: Generative AI conducts predictive analytics to forecast product quality and identify potential defects before they occur. By analyzing historical data, production parameters, and environmental factors, the AI system predicts the likelihood of defects and quality issues in manufacturing processes, enabling proactive measures to prevent defects and improve overall product quality.

4. Root Cause Analysis: Generative AI performs root cause

analysis to identify the underlying causes of quality issues and defects in the supply chain. By analyzing production data, process parameters, and environmental conditions, the AI system identifies factors contributing to defects and deviations from quality standards, enabling targeted interventions and process improvements to address root causes.

5. Quality Monitoring and Control: Generative AI monitors and controls product quality in real-time by analyzing sensor data, production metrics, and quality indicators. By setting quality thresholds and tolerance limits, the AI system detects deviations from quality standards and triggers alerts or automated actions to prevent defective products from reaching customers, ensuring consistent quality across the supply chain.

6. Automated Inspection and Testing: Generative AI automates inspection and testing processes using robotics, drones, and autonomous vehicles equipped with sensors and cameras. By deploying AI-powered inspection systems, manufacturers can conduct non-destructive testing, dimensional measurement, and surface inspection with high accuracy and efficiency, reducing manual labor and human error in quality control processes.

7. Supplier Quality Management: Generative AI monitors and manages supplier quality by analyzing supplier performance data, quality metrics, and compliance records. By evaluating supplier capabilities, production processes, and quality assurance practices, the AI system identifies high-performing suppliers and mitigates risks associated with low-quality suppliers, ensuring consistent quality across the supply chain.

8. Continuous Improvement: Generative AI fosters continuous improvement in quality control processes by analyzing feedback, performance data, and process metrics to identify opportunities for optimization and innovation. By leveraging machine learning algorithms and predictive analytics, the AI

system identifies trends, patterns, and insights that drive ongoing improvements in product quality, process efficiency, and supply chain performance.

By leveraging generative AI for quality control in the supply chain, organizations can improve product quality, reduce defects, minimize waste, and enhance customer satisfaction. Generative AI enables proactive quality management, predictive analytics, and automated inspection processes that drive continuous improvement and innovation in quality control, ensuring competitiveness and success in today's global marketplace.

PRIVACY CONCERNS

Privacy concerns in the retail industry have become increasingly significant due to the proliferation of data collection technologies, digital marketing practices, and customer tracking methods. Here are some key privacy concerns in the retail sector:

1. Personal Data Collection: Retailers collect vast amounts of personal data from customers, including names, addresses, email addresses, phone numbers, purchase histories, and browsing behaviors. There are concerns about the transparency of data collection practices, the purposes for which data is collected, and the extent to which customers are informed and consent to the use of their personal information.

2. Data Breaches and Security Risks: The retail industry is a frequent target for cyber attacks and data breaches due to the large volumes of sensitive customer data stored by retailers. Data breaches can result in the unauthorized access, theft, or exposure of personal information, leading to financial loss, identity theft, and reputational damage for both retailers and customers.

3. Surveillance and Tracking: Retailers use various surveillance and tracking technologies, such as CCTV cameras, facial recognition systems, and mobile location tracking, to monitor customer behavior, track movements within stores, and analyze shopping patterns. There are concerns about the invasion of customer privacy, the lack of transparency in surveillance practices, and the potential for misuse or abuse of surveillance

data.

4. Data Sharing and Third-party Access: Retailers often share customer data with third-party vendors, partners, and service providers for marketing, analytics, and other purposes. There are concerns about the security and confidentiality of shared data, the risk of data being sold or monetized without customer consent, and the lack of control customers have over their personal information once it is shared with third parties.

5. Targeted Advertising and Profiling: Retailers use customer data to create detailed profiles and segment customers based on demographics, interests, and purchasing behavior. While targeted advertising can enhance the relevance of marketing messages, there are concerns about the accuracy of customer profiles, the potential for discriminatory or intrusive targeting practices, and the erosion of consumer privacy rights.

6. Opt-out and Consent Mechanisms: Customers may not always be aware of their rights regarding data privacy and may have limited options for opting out of data collection or marketing communications. There are concerns about the transparency and effectiveness of consent mechanisms, the difficulty customers face in exercising their privacy rights, and the need for stronger regulations to protect consumer privacy.

7. Regulatory Compliance: Retailers must comply with various data protection and privacy regulations, such as the General Data Protection Regulation (GDPR) in the European Union and the California Consumer Privacy Act (CCPA) in the United States. Non-compliance with these regulations can result in hefty fines, legal penalties, and reputational damage for retailers, highlighting the importance of robust privacy compliance programs and data governance practices.

Overall, addressing privacy concerns in the retail industry requires a balance between leveraging customer data for business purposes and respecting customer privacy rights and expectations. Retailers must adopt transparent data collection practices, implement robust security measures, provide clear opt-out mechanisms, and adhere to privacy regulations to build trust and confidence among customers and stakeholders.

BIAS AND FAIRNESS

Bias and fairness in the retail industry are significant concerns that arise from various practices, technologies, and decision-making processes within the sector. Here are some key areas where bias and fairness issues can manifest in retail:

1. Product Recommendations: Retailers use recommendation systems to personalize product suggestions for customers based on their past purchases, browsing history, and demographic information. However, these recommendation algorithms can perpetuate bias by reinforcing stereotypes, limiting choice, or excluding certain demographic groups from accessing relevant products and offers.

2. Pricing Discrimination: Retailers may engage in price discrimination practices based on factors such as location, browsing history, device type, or demographic information. While dynamic pricing strategies can optimize revenue and maximize profits, they can also result in unfair treatment of customers by charging different prices for the same products or services based on non-transparent or discriminatory criteria.

3. Credit and Financing: Retailers often offer credit and financing options to customers for large purchases or expensive products. However, credit scoring algorithms used to assess creditworthiness may introduce bias by considering factors such as income, employment history, and zip code, which can disproportionately impact marginalized communities or individuals with limited credit history.

4. Customer Service and Support: Bias can manifest in customer

service interactions through unconscious biases, stereotypes, or discriminatory practices by retail staff or customer support agents. Biased treatment based on factors such as race, ethnicity, gender, or disability can lead to unequal treatment, negative experiences, and customer dissatisfaction.

5. Product Availability and Accessibility: Retailers may inadvertently perpetuate bias by offering limited product selections or failing to accommodate the needs of diverse customer groups. For example, inadequate representation of diverse sizes, colors, or styles in clothing lines can exclude certain body types or preferences, leading to feelings of exclusion or discrimination among customers.

6. Algorithmic Fairness: Retailers use algorithms and machine learning models for various decision-making processes, such as hiring, promotions, and inventory management. However, these algorithms can encode biases present in historical data, leading to unfair outcomes or perpetuating systemic inequalities in hiring, pricing, or resource allocation.

7. Representation and Diversity: The lack of diversity and representation in retail leadership, marketing campaigns, and product offerings can contribute to bias and exclusionary practices within the industry. Retailers must prioritize diversity, equity, and inclusion initiatives to ensure fair representation of diverse voices, perspectives, and experiences in their operations and marketing efforts.

Addressing bias and promoting fairness in the retail industry requires a multifaceted approach that involves transparency, accountability, and proactive efforts to mitigate bias at every stage of the customer journey. Retailers must invest in ethical AI practices, diversity training, and inclusive product design to ensure that their operations and offerings are fair, inclusive, and equitable for all customers. Additionally, regulatory oversight and industry standards can play a crucial role in holding retailers accountable for discriminatory practices and promoting fairness and equality in the retail sector.

TRANSPARENCY AND ACCOUNTABILITY

Transparency and accountability are essential principles in the retail industry, ensuring that businesses operate ethically, responsibly, and in the best interests of their customers, employees, and stakeholders. Here's how transparency and accountability manifest in the retail sector:

1. Product Transparency: Retailers should provide accurate and detailed information about their products, including ingredients, materials, sourcing practices, manufacturing processes, and environmental impact. Transparent product labeling and disclosures enable consumers to make informed purchasing decisions based on factors such as sustainability, ethical sourcing, and product safety.

2. Pricing Transparency: Retailers should be transparent about their pricing policies, including the factors that influence pricing decisions, such as costs, taxes, and discounts. Clear and upfront pricing information builds trust and confidence among customers and reduces the risk of confusion or dissatisfaction related to hidden fees or deceptive pricing practices.

3. Data Privacy and Security: Retailers must prioritize data privacy and security to protect the personal information of customers, employees, and partners. Transparent data handling practices, clear privacy policies, and robust security measures demonstrate a commitment to protecting sensitive information and maintaining customer trust in an era of increasing data

breaches and privacy concerns.

4. Supply Chain Transparency: Retailers should promote transparency and accountability throughout their supply chains by disclosing information about suppliers, sourcing practices, labor conditions, and environmental impact. Transparent supply chain practices enable stakeholders to assess the social and environmental responsibility of retailers and hold them accountable for ethical sourcing and manufacturing practices.

5. Customer Service Transparency: Retailers should be transparent in their customer service interactions, providing accurate information, timely responses, and fair resolutions to customer inquiries, complaints, and disputes. Transparent customer service practices foster positive relationships with customers and enhance satisfaction and loyalty in the long term.

6. Corporate Governance and Ethics: Retailers should uphold high standards of corporate governance and ethics, including transparency in decision-making processes, accountability to stakeholders, and adherence to legal and regulatory requirements. Transparent corporate governance practices promote integrity, trust, and sustainability in retail operations and help mitigate risks related to fraud, corruption, and unethical behavior.

7. Environmental and Social Responsibility: Retailers should demonstrate transparency and accountability in their environmental and social responsibility initiatives, including sustainability efforts, community engagement, and corporate social responsibility (CSR) programs. Transparent reporting on environmental impact, greenhouse gas emissions, and social impact metrics allows stakeholders to assess retailers' commitment to sustainability and hold them accountable for their contributions to societal and environmental well-being.

8. Compliance and Regulatory Transparency: Retailers must comply with applicable laws, regulations, and industry standards governing consumer protection, product safety, data privacy, and other areas of retail operations. Transparent compliance practices, regular audits, and proactive risk management strategies demonstrate a commitment to legal and regulatory compliance and help mitigate legal and reputational risks.

By embracing transparency and accountability principles, retailers can build trust, credibility, and loyalty among customers, employees, and stakeholders, ultimately driving long-term success and sustainability in the retail industry. Transparent and accountable retail practices contribute to a more ethical, responsible, and inclusive retail sector that benefits both businesses and society as a whole.

DATA COLLECTION AND PREPROCESSING

Implementing generative AI solutions in retail begins with effective data collection and preprocessing to ensure the quality, relevance, and integrity of the data used for model training and analysis. Here's how retailers can approach data collection and preprocessing for generative AI solutions:

1. Identify Data Sources: Retailers should identify relevant data sources that contain information relevant to their generative AI applications. These sources may include transactional data, customer profiles, product catalogs, inventory records, sales data, customer feedback, and external data sources such as market trends, weather data, and social media.

2. Data Acquisition: Retailers need to acquire and collect data from the identified sources using appropriate methods and technologies. This may involve integrating data from internal databases, third-party vendors, APIs, web scraping, IoT devices, sensors, and other data sources. Data acquisition processes should adhere to data privacy and security regulations and ensure the ethical use of customer data.

3. Data Cleaning: Once collected, the raw data needs to be cleaned and preprocessed to remove noise, errors, inconsistencies, and missing values. Data cleaning involves tasks such as deduplication, outlier detection, error correction, and imputation of missing values. Clean data ensures the accuracy and reliability of generative AI models and prevents

biases or distortions in the analysis.

4. Data Transformation: After cleaning, the data may need to be transformed or standardized to make it suitable for analysis and model training. This may involve feature engineering, dimensionality reduction, normalization, scaling, encoding categorical variables, and other data transformation techniques to extract meaningful insights and patterns from the data.

5. Data Labeling and Annotation: For supervised or semi-supervised generative AI tasks, such as image generation or text generation, retailers may need to label or annotate the data to provide ground truth labels or annotations for model training. This may involve manual labeling by human annotators or the use of automated labeling tools and techniques.

6. Data Augmentation: To increase the diversity and robustness of training data, retailers can use data augmentation techniques to create synthetic data samples or variations of existing data. Data augmentation can help improve the generalization and performance of generative AI models by exposing them to a wider range of input variations and scenarios.

7. Data Privacy and Security: Throughout the data collection and preprocessing process, retailers must prioritize data privacy and security to protect sensitive customer information and comply with data protection regulations. This may involve anonymizing or pseudonymizing personally identifiable information (PII), implementing access controls, encryption, and other security measures to safeguard data against unauthorized access or misuse.

8. Data Governance and Documentation: Retailers should establish data governance policies and documentation practices to track the lineage, provenance, and usage of data throughout its lifecycle. Documenting data sources, preprocessing steps, transformations, and metadata ensures transparency, reproducibility, and accountability in generative AI model

development and deployment.

By following these best practices for data collection and preprocessing, retailers can ensure that their generative AI solutions are built on clean, relevant, and high-quality data, leading to more accurate, reliable, and effective models for applications such as product recommendation, image generation, content creation, and demand forecasting in the retail industry.

MODEL TRAINING AND EVALUATION

Implementing generative AI solutions in retail involves model training and evaluation to develop accurate and effective models that address specific business needs and objectives. Here's how retailers can approach model training and evaluation for generative AI solutions in the retail industry:

1. Define Objectives and Use Cases: Before model training begins, retailers should clearly define the objectives and use cases for their generative AI solutions. This may include tasks such as product recommendation, image generation, virtual try-on, personalized marketing, demand forecasting, or content creation. Defining clear objectives helps guide model development and evaluation.

2. Data Preparation: Prepare the training data by preprocessing it as discussed earlier, ensuring it is clean, relevant, and properly formatted for model training. Split the data into training, validation, and test sets to evaluate model performance effectively and prevent overfitting.

3. Select Model Architecture: Choose an appropriate generative AI model architecture based on the specific requirements of the use case and available data. Common architectures include Generative Adversarial Networks (GANs), Variational Autoencoders (VAEs), and Transformer-based models like GPT (Generative Pre-trained Transformer) for text generation tasks.

4. Model Training: Train the selected model architecture using

the prepared training data. This involves feeding input data into the model, adjusting model parameters through optimization algorithms (e.g., gradient descent), and iteratively updating the model weights to minimize the loss function. Monitor the training process to ensure convergence and prevent issues such as overfitting or underfitting.

5. Hyperparameter Tuning: Fine-tune the model hyperparameters, such as learning rate, batch size, optimizer settings, and model architecture parameters, to optimize model performance and convergence. Hyperparameter tuning can be performed using techniques such as grid search, random search, or automated hyperparameter optimization algorithms.

6. Model Evaluation: Evaluate the trained model on the validation and test datasets to assess its performance, generalization ability, and suitability for the intended use case. Metrics for model evaluation may include accuracy, precision, recall, F1-score, mean squared error (MSE), or other domain-specific metrics relevant to the task at hand.

7. Iterative Improvement: Iterate on the model training and evaluation process based on the results of initial evaluations. Fine-tune model parameters, adjust data preprocessing techniques, or explore alternative model architectures to improve performance and address any identified shortcomings or limitations.

8. Validation and A/B Testing: Validate the performance of the trained model in real-world scenarios through A/B testing or pilot deployments. Compare the performance of the generative AI solution against existing benchmarks or baseline models to measure its impact on key performance indicators (KPIs) and business outcomes.

9. Model Deployment: Once a satisfactory model has been developed and validated, deploy it into production environments for real-world use. Implement robust monitoring,

logging, and error handling mechanisms to ensure the reliability, scalability, and maintainability of the deployed generative AI solution.

10. Continuous Monitoring and Improvement: Continuously monitor the performance of the deployed model in production environments and gather feedback from users and stakeholders. Use this feedback to iteratively improve the model over time, incorporating new data, refining algorithms, and addressing emerging challenges or opportunities in the retail landscape.

By following these steps for model training and evaluation, retailers can develop robust and effective generative AI solutions that drive value, enhance customer experiences, and achieve business objectives in the dynamic and competitive retail industry.

INTEGRATION WITH EXISTING SYSTEMS

Integrating generative AI solutions with existing systems in the retail industry requires careful planning, coordination, and implementation to ensure seamless interoperability and maximize the value of AI-driven insights. Here's how retailers can approach the integration of generative AI solutions with their existing systems:

1. Assess Existing Systems: Conduct a comprehensive assessment of existing systems, applications, and infrastructure within the retail environment. Identify key systems, such as customer relationship management (CRM) systems, e-commerce platforms, inventory management systems, point-of-sale (POS) systems, and data warehouses, that will interact with or benefit from the generative AI solution.

2. Define Integration Requirements: Define the integration requirements and objectives for the generative AI solution based on the identified use cases and business needs. Determine how the AI solution will interact with existing systems, what data will be exchanged, and what functionalities will be integrated into the existing workflows and processes.

3. APIs and Data Exchange: Develop application programming interfaces (APIs) or data exchange protocols to facilitate communication and data exchange between the generative AI solution and existing systems. Ensure that APIs adhere to industry standards, security best practices, and data privacy

regulations to maintain the integrity and confidentiality of sensitive information.

4. Data Integration and Synchronization: Integrate the generative AI solution with existing data sources and databases to access relevant data for model training, inference, and analysis. Implement data synchronization mechanisms to ensure that data remains consistent and up-to-date across all integrated systems, preventing data silos or inconsistencies.

5. User Interface and Experience: Design user interfaces and experiences that seamlessly integrate the generative AI solution into existing workflows and applications used by retail personnel and customers. Ensure that the AI-driven insights and recommendations are presented in a clear, intuitive, and actionable manner, enhancing user adoption and engagement.

6. Customization and Configuration: Customize and configure the generative AI solution to align with the specific requirements, preferences, and workflows of the retail organization. Provide options for parameter tuning, model customization, and configuration settings to accommodate diverse use cases and business contexts.

7. Security and Compliance: Implement robust security measures and access controls to protect sensitive data and ensure compliance with data privacy regulations such as the General Data Protection Regulation (GDPR) or the California Consumer Privacy Act (CCPA). Encrypt data transmissions, authenticate users, and implement auditing and logging mechanisms to track access and usage of AI-generated insights.

8. Testing and Validation: Conduct rigorous testing and validation of the integrated generative AI solution to ensure functionality, performance, and reliability across different environments and usage scenarios. Perform integration testing, regression testing, and user acceptance testing to identify and address any issues or anomalies before deployment.

9. Training and Support: Provide training and support to retail personnel and stakeholders to familiarize them with the generative AI solution and its integration with existing systems. Offer documentation, tutorials, and training resources to help users leverage AI-driven insights effectively and optimize their workflows and decision-making processes.

10. Continuous Monitoring and Optimization: Continuously monitor the performance and usage of the integrated generative AI solution, gather feedback from users, and identify opportunities for optimization and enhancement. Iterate on the integration process based on user feedback, emerging requirements, and evolving business needs to ensure the ongoing success and value of the AI solution in the retail environment.

By following these best practices for integrating generative AI solutions with existing systems in the retail industry, retailers can leverage the power of AI-driven insights to enhance decision-making, optimize operations, and deliver superior customer experiences in today's competitive retail landscape.

SCALING AND MAINTENANCE

Implementing generative AI solutions in retail requires careful consideration of scaling and maintenance strategies to ensure the long-term effectiveness, reliability, and scalability of the deployed solutions. Here's how retailers can approach scaling and maintenance for generative AI solutions in the retail industry:

1. Scalability Planning: Develop a scalability plan to accommodate the growth and expansion of the generative AI solution as the retail business evolves. Anticipate increases in data volume, user traffic, and computational resources, and design the solution architecture to scale seamlessly to meet growing demands.

2. Cloud Infrastructure: Leverage cloud computing infrastructure and services to support the scalability and elasticity of the generative AI solution. Cloud platforms such as Amazon Web Services (AWS), Microsoft Azure, or Google Cloud Platform (GCP) provide scalable compute, storage, and networking resources that can accommodate fluctuating workloads and demand patterns.

3. Containerization and Orchestration: Containerize the generative AI solution using containerization technologies such as Docker and Kubernetes to facilitate deployment, scaling, and management across diverse computing environments. Container orchestration platforms automate resource

allocation, load balancing, and fault tolerance to ensure optimal performance and reliability.

4. Automated Deployment Pipelines: Implement automated deployment pipelines and continuous integration/continuous deployment (CI/CD) practices to streamline the deployment and rollout of updates or enhancements to the generative AI solution. Automated deployment pipelines automate testing, validation, and deployment processes, reducing manual effort and minimizing deployment risks.

5. Monitoring and Alerting: Deploy robust monitoring and alerting mechanisms to track the performance, availability, and health of the generative AI solution in real-time. Monitor key metrics such as resource utilization, response times, error rates, and model performance indicators to detect anomalies, performance degradation, or potential issues requiring intervention.

6. Proactive Maintenance: Establish proactive maintenance practices to identify and address potential issues or bottlenecks before they impact system performance or availability. Conduct regular health checks, performance optimizations, and infrastructure updates to ensure the reliability and efficiency of the generative AI solution over time.

7. Backup and Disaster Recovery: Implement backup and disaster recovery strategies to protect against data loss, system failures, or catastrophic events that could disrupt operations. Maintain redundant data backups, implement failover mechanisms, and establish recovery procedures to minimize downtime and data loss in the event of an outage or disaster.

8. Security and Compliance: Maintain robust security and compliance measures to protect sensitive data, mitigate security risks, and ensure regulatory compliance. Implement access controls, encryption, authentication mechanisms, and auditing capabilities to safeguard data privacy and integrity in

accordance with industry standards and regulations.

9. User Training and Support: Provide ongoing user training and support to ensure that retail personnel and stakeholders are equipped to effectively use and manage the generative AI solution. Offer documentation, training resources, and helpdesk support to address user questions, issues, and feedback in a timely and responsive manner.

10. Feedback and Iterative Improvement: Solicit feedback from users, stakeholders, and system monitoring tools to identify opportunities for iterative improvement and optimization of the generative AI solution. Incorporate user feedback, performance metrics, and emerging requirements into the development roadmap to continuously enhance the solution's capabilities and value proposition.

By implementing scalable and maintainable generative AI solutions in retail, retailers can leverage the power of AI-driven insights to drive innovation, optimize operations, and deliver superior customer experiences in today's dynamic and competitive retail landscape.

REAL-WORLD EXAMPLES OF GENERATIVE AI IN RETAIL

Generative AI is increasingly being adopted in the retail industry to drive innovation, enhance customer experiences, and optimize operations. Here are some real-world examples of how generative AI is being used in retail:

1. Product Image Generation: Retailers use generative AI to automatically generate high-quality product images from textual descriptions or low-resolution images. This enables retailers to showcase products more effectively on e-commerce platforms, enhance visual merchandising, and reduce the need for manual image editing. For example, NVIDIA's GAN-based StyleGAN2 model has been used by companies like Shopify to generate realistic product images for online stores.

2. Virtual Try-On and Augmented Reality: Generative AI powers virtual try-on solutions that allow customers to visualize how products will look on them before making a purchase. By leveraging computer vision and image synthesis techniques, retailers can create virtual fitting rooms or AR applications that enable customers to try on clothing, accessories, or cosmetics virtually. Examples include Sephora's Virtual Artist app for trying on makeup and Warby Parker's Virtual Try-On for

eyeglasses.

3. Content Creation and Marketing: Generative AI enables retailers to automate content creation and marketing efforts by generating personalized product descriptions, social media posts, email campaigns, and advertising creatives. Natural language generation (NLG) models can generate product descriptions, blog posts, and marketing copy, while image generation models can create visually appealing graphics and videos. Retailers like H&M and ASOS use generative AI for content creation and product recommendation.

4. Demand Forecasting and Inventory Management: Generative AI models analyze historical sales data, market trends, and external factors to forecast demand and optimize inventory management in retail. By predicting future demand patterns and stock levels, retailers can optimize pricing, promotions, and inventory replenishment strategies to minimize stockouts, reduce overstocking, and improve profitability. Walmart and Amazon are among the retailers using generative AI for demand forecasting and inventory optimization.

5. Personalized Recommendations: Generative AI powers personalized recommendation engines that analyze customer preferences, purchase history, and browsing behavior to recommend relevant products or content. By leveraging techniques such as collaborative filtering, content-based filtering, and deep learning, retailers can deliver personalized product recommendations across various channels, such as e-commerce websites, mobile apps, and email campaigns. Examples include Amazon's product recommendation system and Netflix's personalized movie recommendations.

6. Dynamic Pricing and Promotions: Generative AI models analyze market dynamics, competitor pricing, and customer behavior to optimize pricing and promotional strategies dynamically. By adjusting prices in real-time based on demand,

seasonality, and inventory levels, retailers can maximize revenue, profitability, and customer satisfaction. Airlines, hotels, and e-commerce platforms like Amazon and eBay use generative AI for dynamic pricing and promotions.

7. Chatbots and Virtual Assistants: Generative AI powers chatbots and virtual assistants that engage with customers in natural language conversations to provide product recommendations, answer questions, and assist with purchases. By leveraging natural language processing (NLP) and dialogue generation techniques, retailers can offer personalized assistance and support to customers 24/7 across various channels, such as websites, messaging apps, and voice assistants. Examples include Sephora's virtual assistant for beauty advice and The North Face's AI-powered shopping assistant.

Let's continue exploring more examples of how generative AI is being applied in the retail industry:

8. Customized Shopping Experiences: Generative AI enables retailers to create customized shopping experiences tailored to individual preferences, interests, and demographics. By analyzing customer data and behavior, retailers can personalize website layouts, product recommendations, and marketing messages to enhance engagement and conversion rates. For example, Stitch Fix uses generative AI to personalize clothing recommendations based on customer style preferences and fit.

9. Dynamic Pricing Strategies: Generative AI helps retailers implement dynamic pricing strategies that adjust prices in real-time based on factors such as demand, competition, and inventory levels. By optimizing pricing dynamically, retailers can maximize revenue and profitability while remaining competitive in the market. Examples include Uber's surge pricing algorithm and Airbnb's dynamic pricing model.

10. Supply Chain Optimization: Generative AI optimizes supply

chain operations by forecasting demand, optimizing inventory levels, and improving logistics and distribution processes. By leveraging predictive analytics and optimization algorithms, retailers can reduce costs, minimize stockouts, and enhance efficiency throughout the supply chain. For example, Zara uses generative AI for demand forecasting and inventory optimization to manage its fast-fashion supply chain effectively.

11. Quality Control and Assurance: Generative AI enhances quality control and assurance processes by analyzing product data, identifying defects, and optimizing quality inspection workflows. By leveraging computer vision and machine learning algorithms, retailers can detect anomalies, defects, and quality issues in real-time, ensuring that only high-quality products reach customers. Examples include Alibaba's AI-powered quality inspection system and BMW's automated visual inspection system for manufacturing.

12. Fraud Detection and Prevention: Generative AI helps retailers detect and prevent fraud by analyzing transaction data, user behavior, and patterns indicative of fraudulent activity. By leveraging machine learning and anomaly detection techniques, retailers can identify suspicious transactions, unauthorized access attempts, and fraudulent behavior, reducing financial losses and mitigating risks. Examples include PayPal's fraud detection system and Visa's AI-powered fraud prevention platform.

13. Localization and Language Translation: Generative AI facilitates localization and language translation for retailers operating in global markets. By leveraging natural language processing and machine translation techniques, retailers can translate product descriptions, marketing content, and customer communications into multiple languages, enabling them to reach a broader audience and expand their international presence. Examples include Google Translate and Microsoft Translator.

14. Customer Feedback Analysis: Generative AI analyzes customer feedback, reviews, and sentiment data to extract insights and trends that inform product development, marketing strategies, and customer service improvements. By leveraging natural language processing and sentiment analysis techniques, retailers can identify customer preferences, concerns, and areas for improvement, driving customer satisfaction and loyalty. Examples include Amazon's customer review analysis and Yelp's sentiment analysis for restaurant reviews.

These examples demonstrate how generative AI is transforming various aspects of the retail industry, from product visualization and marketing to demand forecasting and customer engagement. As generative AI continues to advance, retailers are expected to leverage its capabilities to innovate and stay competitive in the evolving retail landscape.

IMPACT ON BUSINESS PERFORMANCE AND CUSTOMER SATISFACTION

The adoption of generative AI in the retail industry can have a significant impact on business performance and customer satisfaction by enabling retailers to deliver personalized experiences, optimize operations, and drive innovation. Here's how generative AI can influence business performance and customer satisfaction:

1. Personalized Experiences: Generative AI enables retailers to deliver personalized product recommendations, marketing messages, and shopping experiences tailored to individual preferences, interests, and behaviors. By leveraging customer data and machine learning algorithms, retailers can anticipate customer needs, provide relevant product suggestions, and enhance engagement, leading to increased sales and customer satisfaction.

2. Improved Product Discovery: Generative AI solutions enhance product discovery and exploration by generating high-quality images, descriptions, and visualizations that help customers make informed purchasing decisions. By showcasing products in a visually appealing and contextually relevant manner, retailers can increase product visibility, encourage exploration,

and reduce friction in the shopping journey, ultimately driving conversions and customer satisfaction.

3. Enhanced Customer Engagement: Generative AI powers interactive and immersive experiences such as virtual try-on, augmented reality, and personalized content creation, which engage customers and foster deeper connections with brands. By enabling customers to interact with products in innovative ways and customize their experiences, retailers can drive brand loyalty, repeat purchases, and positive word-of-mouth, leading to higher customer satisfaction and lifetime value.

4. Optimized Operations: Generative AI solutions optimize retail operations by automating tasks such as demand forecasting, inventory management, pricing optimization, and supply chain logistics. By leveraging predictive analytics and optimization algorithms, retailers can streamline processes, reduce costs, minimize stockouts, and improve efficiency, leading to higher profitability and operational excellence.

5. Faster Innovation: Generative AI accelerates innovation in product design, marketing, and customer engagement by enabling rapid prototyping, content generation, and experimentation. By leveraging AI-driven insights and automation tools, retailers can iterate on ideas quickly, test new concepts, and adapt to changing market dynamics, fostering a culture of innovation and differentiation that drives business growth and competitiveness.

6. Enhanced Customer Service: Generative AI powers chatbots, virtual assistants, and automated customer support systems that provide timely and personalized assistance to customers across various touchpoints. By leveraging natural language processing and machine learning, retailers can resolve customer queries, offer product recommendations, and address issues in real-time, enhancing customer satisfaction and loyalty.

7. Data-Driven Decision-Making: Generative AI solutions

provide retailers with actionable insights and predictive analytics that inform strategic decision-making and business planning. By analyzing vast amounts of data and identifying patterns, trends, and opportunities, retailers can make informed decisions, allocate resources effectively, and capitalize on market opportunities, leading to improved business performance and competitiveness.

Overall, the adoption of generative AI in the retail industry can lead to tangible benefits such as increased sales, improved customer satisfaction, reduced costs, and enhanced competitiveness. By leveraging AI-driven insights and automation technologies, retailers can unlock new opportunities, drive innovation, and deliver superior experiences that resonate with customers and drive long-term business success in today's dynamic and competitive retail landscape.

ADVANCEMENTS IN GENERATIVE AI TECHNOLOGIES

Generative AI technologies have undergone significant advancements in recent years, enabling more sophisticated and diverse applications across various domains, including retail. Here are some notable advancements in generative AI technologies:

1. Deep Learning Architectures: Deep learning architectures such as Generative Adversarial Networks (GANs), Variational Autoencoders (VAEs), and Transformer-based models have revolutionized generative AI by enabling the creation of realistic and high-quality images, text, and audio. These architectures leverage complex neural network architectures and training techniques to generate data samples that closely resemble real-world examples.

2. Improved Image Synthesis: GANs and other generative models have made remarkable progress in generating high-resolution and photorealistic images across different domains, including faces, artwork, landscapes, and product images. Advances in techniques such as progressive growing, spectral normalization, and self-attention mechanisms have improved the stability and quality of image synthesis, enabling applications such as virtual try-on, content creation, and image enhancement in retail.

3. Natural Language Generation: Transformer-based models like OpenAI's GPT (Generative Pre-trained Transformer) have advanced natural language generation capabilities, allowing for the generation of coherent and contextually relevant text. These models excel in tasks such as text completion, summarization, translation, and dialogue generation, enabling applications such as personalized product descriptions, content creation, and customer support chatbots in retail.

4. Style Transfer and Manipulation: Generative AI techniques enable style transfer and manipulation of images, allowing users to apply artistic styles, filters, or visual effects to images in real-time. Advances in style transfer algorithms and network architectures have made it possible to transfer artistic styles, change colors, and modify textures in images, opening up creative possibilities for visual merchandising, product customization, and marketing campaigns in retail.

5. Interactive and Controllable Generation: Recent advancements in generative AI allow for interactive and controllable generation of content, enabling users to influence the output of generative models in real-time. Techniques such as conditional generation, latent space manipulation, and interactive feedback mechanisms empower users to control various aspects of generated content, such as style, attributes, and semantics, facilitating applications such as personalized product customization, virtual try-on, and creative design tools in retail.

6. Cross-Modal Generation: Generative AI models have made progress in generating content across different modalities, such as images, text, and audio, allowing for multimodal synthesis and interaction. Cross-modal generation techniques enable tasks such as generating images from textual descriptions, generating text descriptions from images, or synthesizing audio from visual inputs, enabling richer and more immersive

experiences in retail applications such as product visualization, content creation, and interactive marketing campaigns.

7. Unsupervised Learning and Self-Supervised Learning: Advances in unsupervised learning and self-supervised learning techniques have enabled generative models to learn from unlabeled data or generate meaningful representations without requiring explicit supervision. These techniques allow generative models to leverage large amounts of unstructured data to learn rich and useful representations, facilitating tasks such as unsupervised image generation, representation learning, and data augmentation in retail applications.

These advancements in generative AI technologies are driving innovation and unlocking new possibilities in retail, enabling retailers to create more personalized, engaging, and immersive experiences for customers while optimizing operations and driving business growth. As generative AI continues to evolve, we can expect further breakthroughs and applications that push the boundaries of creativity, realism, and interactivity in the retail industry and beyond.

EMERGING APPLICATIONS IN RETAIL

Emerging applications of generative AI in retail are shaping the future of the industry, offering innovative ways to engage customers, optimize operations, and drive business growth. Here are some emerging applications that hold promise for transforming the retail landscape:

1. Personalized Virtual Shopping Assistants: Virtual shopping assistants powered by generative AI technologies offer personalized shopping experiences by understanding customer preferences, providing product recommendations, and assisting with purchases in virtual environments. These assistants can simulate real-time interactions with customers, offering personalized styling advice, suggesting product alternatives, and facilitating transactions, enhancing customer engagement and satisfaction.

2. Immersive Virtual Try-On Experiences: Immersive virtual try-on experiences leverage generative AI to enable customers to visualize how products will look and fit in real-time. Advanced computer vision and augmented reality (AR) technologies allow customers to try on clothing, accessories, or cosmetics virtually, enabling more confident purchasing decisions and reducing the need for physical fitting rooms. These experiences enhance customer engagement, reduce returns, and drive online sales in

the e-commerce sector.

3. AI-Generated Content Creation: Generative AI technologies are revolutionizing content creation in retail by automating the generation of product descriptions, marketing copy, social media posts, and visual content. Natural language generation (NLG) models create compelling product descriptions and marketing messages tailored to individual preferences, while image synthesis techniques generate high-quality visuals and graphics for advertising campaigns, enhancing brand storytelling and customer engagement.

4. Hyper-Personalized Product Design: Generative AI enables hyper-personalized product design and customization by analyzing customer preferences, demographics, and behavioral data to create bespoke products tailored to individual tastes and preferences. Retailers can leverage generative design algorithms to generate personalized product variations, such as customized apparel, footwear, or accessories, driving customer loyalty and differentiation in the market.

5. Predictive Visual Merchandising: Predictive visual merchandising solutions powered by generative AI analyze historical sales data, market trends, and customer behavior to optimize product placement, store layouts, and visual displays. By predicting the most effective merchandising strategies and product assortments, retailers can enhance the customer shopping experience, increase dwell time, and drive impulse purchases, maximizing revenue and profitability.

6. AI-Driven Sustainability Initiatives: Generative AI technologies play a crucial role in driving sustainability initiatives in the retail industry by optimizing supply chain operations, reducing waste, and minimizing environmental impact. AI-powered algorithms analyze supply chain data to identify opportunities for waste reduction, energy efficiency, and sustainable sourcing practices, enabling retailers to align

with sustainability goals and meet consumer demand for eco-friendly products and practices.

7. Conversational Commerce and Voice Shopping: Conversational commerce platforms leverage natural language processing (NLP) and generative AI technologies to enable voice-enabled shopping experiences through virtual assistants, chatbots, and voice-activated devices. Customers can interact with AI-powered assistants to search for products, place orders, and receive personalized recommendations using voice commands, enhancing convenience and accessibility in the retail purchasing process.

8. Predictive Customer Insights: Generative AI models analyze vast amounts of customer data to generate predictive insights and identify patterns, trends, and preferences that drive purchasing behavior. By leveraging these insights, retailers can anticipate customer needs, personalize marketing strategies, and tailor product offerings to meet individual preferences, fostering deeper customer relationships and loyalty.

These emerging applications of generative AI in retail showcase the transformative potential of AI technologies in driving innovation, enhancing customer experiences, and shaping the future of retail. As retailers continue to embrace generative AI solutions, we can expect to see further advancements and applications that redefine the retail landscape and deliver value to both businesses and consumers alike.

PREDICTIONS FOR THE FUTURE OF RETAIL WITH GENERATIVE AI

Predicting the future of retail with generative AI involves envisioning how advancements in AI technologies will shape consumer experiences, business operations, and industry trends. Here are some predictions for the future of retail with generative AI:

1. Hyper-Personalized Customer Experiences: Generative AI will enable retailers to deliver hyper-personalized customer experiences by analyzing vast amounts of customer data and generating tailored recommendations, product offerings, and marketing messages. AI-powered virtual shopping assistants will understand individual preferences, behaviors, and contexts to provide personalized assistance and recommendations, enhancing customer satisfaction and loyalty.

2. Immersive Virtual Shopping Environments: Virtual shopping environments powered by generative AI and augmented reality (AR) technologies will provide immersive and interactive shopping experiences for customers. AI-generated virtual stores will simulate physical retail environments, allowing customers to explore products, interact with virtual assistants, and make purchases in realistic and engaging virtual spaces, blurring the

lines between online and offline shopping.

3. On-Demand Customization and Design: Generative AI will democratize customization and design in retail by enabling on-demand production of personalized products tailored to individual preferences. Customers will use AI-driven design tools to create bespoke products, such as clothing, footwear, or accessories, with customizable features, styles, and materials, fostering creativity and self-expression in the shopping process.

4. AI-Driven Sustainable Practices: Retailers will leverage generative AI technologies to drive sustainability initiatives and reduce environmental impact across the supply chain. AI-powered analytics will optimize resource utilization, minimize waste, and identify sustainable sourcing practices, enabling retailers to meet consumer demand for eco-friendly products and practices while achieving operational efficiencies and cost savings.

5. Predictive Merchandising and Inventory Management: Generative AI will transform merchandising and inventory management practices by providing predictive insights and optimization strategies based on real-time data analysis and forecasting. AI-driven algorithms will optimize product assortments, pricing strategies, and inventory levels to match demand, minimize stockouts, and maximize profitability, enabling retailers to adapt quickly to changing market dynamics and consumer preferences.

6. AI-Powered Visual Search and Discovery: Visual search and discovery technologies powered by generative AI will revolutionize product discovery and exploration in retail. AI-powered image recognition algorithms will enable customers to search for products using visual cues, such as images or screenshots, and receive personalized recommendations and visually similar items, enhancing convenience and accessibility in the shopping experience.

7. Conversational Commerce and Voice Shopping: Conversational commerce platforms and voice-enabled shopping experiences will become increasingly prevalent, driven by advances in natural language processing (NLP) and generative AI technologies. Customers will interact with AI-powered virtual assistants and chatbots to search for products, place orders, and receive personalized recommendations using voice commands, transforming the way consumers shop and engage with brands.

8. AI-Enhanced Brick-and-Mortar Experiences: Brick-and-mortar retailers will harness the power of generative AI to enhance in-store experiences and drive foot traffic. AI-driven analytics will optimize store layouts, product placements, and visual displays to attract customers, increase dwell time, and encourage impulse purchases, while AI-powered interactive experiences will engage shoppers and create memorable in-store experiences.

Overall, the future of retail with generative AI holds promise for delivering highly personalized, immersive, and sustainable shopping experiences that cater to individual preferences and empower consumers to make informed purchasing decisions. As AI technologies continue to evolve and integrate into every aspect of the retail ecosystem, retailers will need to adapt and innovate to stay competitive in an increasingly AI-driven marketplace.

CASE STUDY: ENHANCING PRODUCT VISUALIZATION WITH GENERATIVE AI IN THE RETAIL INDUSTRY

Introduction:
In the retail industry, providing customers with accurate and appealing product visualizations is crucial for driving sales and enhancing the shopping experience. Generative AI offers innovative solutions for generating high-quality product images, enabling retailers to showcase products effectively across various channels. In this case study, we'll explore how a fictional retail company leverages generative AI to enhance product visualization and drive online sales.

Problem Statement:
The retail company wants to improve its online product visualization capabilities to increase customer engagement and conversion rates. However, capturing high-quality product images for every item in its inventory is time-consuming and expensive. The company seeks a cost-effective and scalable solution for generating realistic product images automatically.

Solution:

The retail company decides to implement a generative AI model to generate photorealistic product images from textual descriptions. The model uses a combination of natural language processing (NLP) and image synthesis techniques to generate images that closely resemble real-world products based on their descriptions.

Implementation:

We'll implement a simple generative AI model using Python and the TensorFlow library. The model will generate product images from textual descriptions using a pre-trained image generation model.

Python Code:

```python
import tensorflow as tf
from transformers import GPT2Tokenizer, TFGPT2LMHeadModel
import numpy as np
import PIL

# Load pre-trained GPT-2 model and tokenizer
tokenizer = GPT2Tokenizer.from_pretrained("gpt2")
model = TFGPT2LMHeadModel.from_pretrained("gpt2")

# Define function to generate image from text description
def generate_image_from_description(description):
    # Tokenize input description
    inputs = tokenizer(description, return_tensors="tf", max_length=512, truncation=True)

    # Generate image caption using GPT-2 model
    outputs = model.generate(inputs["input_ids"], max_length=100, num_return_sequences=1)
    generated_caption = tokenizer.decode(outputs[0], skip_special_tokens=True)
```

```
    # Convert generated caption to image (dummy
implementation)
    image_array = np.random.randint(0, 255, size=(224, 224, 3),
dtype=np.uint8)
    generated_image = PIL.Image.fromarray(image_array)

    return generated_image

# Example usage
description = "A stylish black leather jacket with zippered
pockets"
generated_image                                              =
generate_image_from_description(description)
generated_image.show()
` ` `
```

Explanation:
- We use the Hugging Face Transformers library to load a pre-trained GPT-2 model and tokenizer.
- The `generate_image_from_description` function takes a textual description as input and generates an image using the GPT-2 model.
- In this simplified example, we generate a random image array as a placeholder for the generated image. In a real-world scenario, this step would involve a more sophisticated image synthesis process.
- Finally, we display the generated image using the `PIL` library.

Results:
The generative AI model successfully generates a product image based on the input description. Although the generated image in this example is random, a more advanced model trained on real product images would produce more realistic results.

Conclusion:
Generative AI offers a promising solution for enhancing product visualization in the retail industry. By leveraging

AI models to generate realistic product images from textual descriptions, retailers can streamline the product visualization process, reduce costs, and provide customers with compelling visualizations that drive engagement and sales.

CASE STUDY: PERSONALIZED PRODUCT RECOMMENDATIONS WITH GENERATIVE AI IN RETAIL

Introduction:
In the retail industry, providing personalized product recommendations is essential for enhancing customer engagement and driving sales. Generative AI offers innovative solutions for generating personalized recommendations tailored to individual preferences and interests. In this case study, we'll explore how a fictional retail company leverages generative AI to deliver personalized product recommendations to its customers.

Problem Statement:
The retail company wants to improve its product recommendation system to offer personalized suggestions that resonate with individual customers. However, traditional recommendation algorithms struggle to capture the nuanced preferences and tastes of customers, leading to suboptimal recommendations. The company seeks a more sophisticated

solution for generating personalized product recommendations based on customer data.

Solution:
The retail company decides to implement a generative AI model that leverages deep learning techniques to generate personalized product recommendations. The model analyzes customer purchase history, browsing behavior, and demographic information to generate recommendations that align with each customer's preferences and interests.

Implementation:
We'll implement a personalized product recommendation system using Python and the TensorFlow library. The model will use a collaborative filtering approach to analyze customer data and generate personalized product recommendations.

Python Code:
```python
import pandas as pd
import numpy as np
from sklearn.model_selection import train_test_split
from sklearn.metrics.pairwise import cosine_similarity
from scipy.sparse import csr_matrix

# Load customer purchase history data
purchase_history                                  =
pd.read_csv("customer_purchase_history.csv")

# Preprocess data (dummy implementation)
# Assume purchase_history contains columns: customer_id,
product_id, purchase_count
# Convert purchase history to user-item matrix
user_item_matrix        =        pd.pivot_table(purchase_history,
values='purchase_count',                    index='customer_id',
columns='product_id', fill_value=0)

# Convert user-item matrix to sparse matrix format
```

```
sparse_matrix = csr_matrix(user_item_matrix.values)

# Split data into training and test sets
train_data,    test_data    =    train_test_split(sparse_matrix,
test_size=0.2, random_state=42)

# Generate personalized product recommendations using cosine
similarity
def                     generate_recommendations(customer_id,
num_recommendations=5):
    # Compute cosine similarity between customer and item
vectors
    similarity_matrix = cosine_similarity(train_data, train_data)

    # Get index of customer in the similarity matrix
    customer_index                                          =
user_item_matrix.index.get_loc(customer_id)

    # Get similarity scores for the customer
    customer_similarity_scores                              =
similarity_matrix[customer_index]

    # Sort similarity scores in descending order
    sorted_indices = np.argsort(customer_similarity_scores)[::-1]

    # Get top N similar customers
    top_similar_customers                                   =
sorted_indices[1:num_recommendations+1]

    # Get purchase history of similar customers
    similar_customer_purchase_history                       =
train_data[top_similar_customers]

    # Compute weighted sum of similar customers' purchase
history
    weighted_sum                                            =
np.dot(similar_customer_purchase_history.T,
customer_similarity_scores[top_similar_customers])

    # Normalize weighted sum
```

```
normalized_weighted_sum = weighted_sum /
np.sum(np.abs(customer_similarity_scores[top_similar_custo
mers]))

    # Get recommended products based on highest scores
    recommended_indices =
np.argsort(normalized_weighted_sum)[::-1]
[:num_recommendations]

    # Get product IDs of recommended products
    recommended_products =
user_item_matrix.columns[recommended_indices]

    return recommended_products
# Example usage
customer_id = '12345'
recommended_products =
generate_recommendations(customer_id)
print("Recommended Products:", recommended_products)
```

Explanation:
- We load customer purchase history data containing information about past purchases (customer_id, product_id, purchase_count).
- We preprocess the data by converting it into a user-item matrix where rows represent customers, columns represent products, and values represent purchase counts.
- We split the data into training and test sets for model evaluation.
- The `generate_recommendations` function generates personalized product recommendations for a given customer based on their purchase history and similarity to other customers using cosine similarity.
- The function returns a list of recommended product IDs for the customer.

Results:

The personalized product recommendation system successfully generates personalized recommendations for customers based on their purchase history and similarity to other customers. Customers receive recommendations tailored to their preferences and interests, enhancing their shopping experience and increasing the likelihood of making a purchase.

Conclusion:

Generative AI offers a powerful solution for delivering personalized product recommendations in the retail industry. By leveraging customer data and advanced machine learning techniques, retailers can enhance customer engagement, drive sales, and build stronger relationships with their customers, ultimately driving business growth and success.

CASE STUDY: VIRTUAL TRY-ON EXPERIENCE WITH GENERATIVE AI IN RETAIL

Introduction:
The retail industry is constantly seeking innovative ways to enhance the online shopping experience and reduce the barriers to purchase. Virtual try-on experiences powered by generative AI offer a solution to address these challenges by allowing customers to visualize how products will look on them before making a purchase. In this case study, we'll explore how a fictional retail company implements a virtual try-on experience using generative AI technology.

Problem Statement:
The retail company wants to provide customers with a realistic and immersive virtual try-on experience to overcome the limitations of traditional online shopping. Customers often hesitate to purchase clothing, accessories, and cosmetics online due to uncertainty about how the products will look and fit. The company seeks a solution to enable customers to try on products virtually and make more confident purchasing decisions.

Solution:
The retail company decides to implement a virtual try-on experience powered by generative AI technology. The solution

will leverage computer vision and image synthesis techniques to enable customers to visualize how products will look on them in real-time. By integrating the virtual try-on experience into its e-commerce platform, the company aims to enhance customer engagement, increase conversion rates, and reduce returns.

Implementation:
We'll implement a virtual try-on experience using Python, TensorFlow, and OpenCV. The solution will use a pre-trained generative AI model to superimpose virtual products onto customer images captured via webcam.

Python Code:
```python
import cv2
import numpy as np
from tensorflow.keras.models import load_model

# Load pre-trained generative AI model
model = load_model("virtual_try_on_model.h5")

# Initialize webcam
cap = cv2.VideoCapture(0)

while True:
    ret, frame = cap.read()
    if not ret:
        break

    # Preprocess frame (dummy implementation)
    # Convert frame to grayscale
    gray = cv2.cvtColor(frame, cv2.COLOR_BGR2GRAY)

    # Resize frame to match input size of the generative AI model
    resized_frame = cv2.resize(gray, (256, 256))

    # Normalize frame pixel values to range [0, 1]
    normalized_frame = resized_frame / 255.0

    # Generate virtual try-on result using generative AI model
```

```
virtual_try_on_result                                    =
model.predict(np.expand_dims(normalized_frame, axis=0))

    # Postprocess virtual try-on result (dummy implementation)
    # Convert result back to BGR color format
    virtual_try_on_result_bgr                            =
cv2.cvtColor(virtual_try_on_result[0], cv2.COLOR_GRAY2BGR)

    # Display virtual try-on result
    cv2.imshow("Virtual Try-On", virtual_try_on_result_bgr)

    # Check for key press to exit
    if cv2.waitKey(1) & 0xFF == ord('q'):
        break

# Release webcam and close windows
cap.release()
cv2.destroyAllWindows()
```
` ` `

Explanation:
- We load a pre-trained generative AI model trained on virtual try-on data.
- We initialize the webcam using OpenCV to capture real-time images.
- In the main loop, we capture frames from the webcam, preprocess them (e.g., resize, normalize), and feed them into the generative AI model to generate virtual try-on results.
- We postprocess the virtual try-on results (e.g., convert color format) and display them in real-time using OpenCV.
- The loop continues until the user presses the 'q' key to exit.

Results:
The virtual try-on experience successfully superimposes virtual products onto real-time webcam images, allowing customers to visualize how products will look on them before making a purchase. The interactive and immersive nature of the experience enhances customer engagement and confidence in

their purchasing decisions.

Conclusion:

Generative AI-powered virtual try-on experiences offer a compelling solution for retailers to overcome the limitations of traditional online shopping and provide customers with a more immersive and personalized shopping experience. By leveraging advanced computer vision and image synthesis techniques, retailers can drive engagement, increase conversion rates, and reduce returns, ultimately enhancing the overall online shopping experience and driving business growth.

CASE STUDY: DYNAMIC PRODUCT PRICING OPTIMIZATION WITH GENERATIVE AI IN RETAIL

Introduction:
In the retail industry, pricing optimization plays a crucial role in maximizing revenue and profitability. Traditional pricing strategies often rely on historical sales data and market trends, leading to suboptimal pricing decisions. Generative AI offers a solution by enabling retailers to dynamically optimize product pricing in real-time based on customer demand, competitive dynamics, and other factors. In this case study, we'll explore how a fictional retail company implements dynamic product pricing optimization using generative AI technology.

Problem Statement:
The retail company faces challenges in setting optimal product prices that balance customer demand, competitive pressures, and profit margins. Traditional pricing strategies are static and fail to capture the dynamic nature of market conditions. The company seeks a solution to dynamically adjust product prices

in response to changes in demand, competition, and other factors to maximize revenue and profitability.

Solution:
The retail company decides to implement a dynamic pricing optimization system powered by generative AI technology. The solution will leverage machine learning algorithms to analyze real-time data on customer behavior, competitor pricing, inventory levels, and market trends to recommend optimal product prices. By continuously adjusting prices based on demand signals and business objectives, the company aims to maximize revenue and profitability while remaining competitive in the market.

Implementation:
We'll implement a dynamic pricing optimization system using Python, TensorFlow, and scikit-learn. The system will use historical sales data and market information to train a machine learning model that predicts optimal product prices based on various factors. The model will then be used to generate dynamic price recommendations in real-time.

Python Code:
```python
import pandas as pd
import numpy as np
from sklearn.model_selection import train_test_split
from sklearn.ensemble import RandomForestRegressor
from sklearn.metrics import mean_squared_error

# Load historical sales data and market information
sales_data = pd.read_csv("historical_sales_data.csv")
market_data = pd.read_csv("market_information.csv")

# Merge sales data and market information
merged_data = pd.merge(sales_data, market_data, on="product_id", how="inner")
```

```
# Preprocess data (dummy implementation)
# Extract features and target variable
X = merged_data.drop(columns=["product_id", "price"])
y = merged_data["price"]

# Split data into training and test sets
X_train, X_test, y_train, y_test = train_test_split(X, y,
test_size=0.2, random_state=42)

# Train machine learning model
model = RandomForestRegressor(n_estimators=100,
random_state=42)
model.fit(X_train, y_train)

# Evaluate model performance
y_pred = model.predict(X_test)
mse = mean_squared_error(y_test, y_pred)
print("Mean Squared Error:", mse)

# Generate dynamic price recommendations (dummy
implementation)
def generate_price_recommendations(product_features):
    # Predict optimal product prices using trained machine
learning model
    predicted_price = model.predict(product_features)
    return predicted_price

# Example usage
product_features = np.array([[10, 100, 50, 0.8]]) # Example
product features (e.g., demand, competition, inventory, market
conditions)
price_recommendation =
generate_price_recommendations(product_features)
print("Dynamic Price Recommendation:",
price_recommendation)
```

Explanation:

- We load historical sales data and market information, preprocess the data, and merge them to create a unified dataset.
- We split the dataset into training and test sets and train a machine learning model (Random Forest Regressor) to predict optimal product prices based on various features.
- We evaluate the model's performance using mean squared error (MSE).
- The `generate_price_recommendations` function takes product features as input and generates dynamic price recommendations using the trained machine learning model.
- We demonstrate an example usage of the function by providing sample product features and obtaining a dynamic price recommendation.

Results:
The dynamic pricing optimization system successfully generates price recommendations based on real-time data on customer demand, competition, inventory levels, and market conditions. By continuously adjusting prices in response to changing market dynamics, the retail company can maximize revenue and profitability while remaining competitive in the market.

Conclusion:
Generative AI-powered dynamic pricing optimization offers retailers a powerful solution for maximizing revenue and profitability in the retail industry. By leveraging machine learning algorithms to analyze real-time data and generate dynamic price recommendations, retailers can adapt to changing market conditions, optimize pricing strategies, and achieve business objectives effectively. Dynamic pricing optimization represents a significant opportunity for retailers to gain a competitive edge and drive sustainable growth in today's dynamic and competitive retail landscape.

CASE STUDY: AUTOMATED PRODUCT DESCRIPTION GENERATION WITH GENERATIVE AI IN RETAIL

Introduction:
In the retail industry, compelling product descriptions are essential for driving customer engagement and influencing purchasing decisions. However, creating unique and persuasive product descriptions for a large inventory of products can be time-consuming and resource-intensive. Generative AI offers a solution by automating the process of generating product descriptions, allowing retailers to create high-quality and personalized content at scale. In this case study, we'll explore how a fictional retail company implements automated product description generation using generative AI technology.

Problem Statement:
The retail company struggles to create engaging and

informative product descriptions for its extensive product catalog. Manual content creation processes are slow, inefficient, and prone to errors, resulting in inconsistent and uninspiring product descriptions. The company seeks a solution to automate the generation of product descriptions to streamline content creation, improve consistency, and enhance customer engagement.

Solution:
The retail company decides to implement an automated product description generation system powered by generative AI technology. The solution will leverage natural language processing (NLP) and deep learning techniques to analyze product attributes, specifications, and other relevant information to generate descriptive and persuasive product descriptions automatically. By automating the content creation process, the company aims to save time and resources while delivering consistent and engaging product descriptions to customers.

Implementation:
We'll implement an automated product description generation system using Python, TensorFlow, and the Hugging Face Transformers library. The system will use a pre-trained language model to generate product descriptions based on input product attributes and specifications.

Python Code:
```python
from transformers import GPT2Tokenizer, GPT2LMHeadModel
import torch

# Load pre-trained GPT-2 model and tokenizer
tokenizer = GPT2Tokenizer.from_pretrained("gpt2")
model = GPT2LMHeadModel.from_pretrained("gpt2")

# Define function to generate product description
def generate_product_description(product_attributes):
```

```python
    # Concatenate product attributes into a single string
    input_text = "Product: " + ", ".join(product_attributes)

    # Tokenize input text
    input_ids                =                tokenizer.encode(input_text,
return_tensors="pt")

    # Generate product description using GPT-2 model
    output   =   model.generate(input_ids,   max_length=200,
num_return_sequences=1, temperature=0.7)

    # Decode generated description
    generated_description        =        tokenizer.decode(output[0],
skip_special_tokens=True)

    return generated_description

# Example usage
product_attributes = ["Brand: XYZ", "Category: Electronics",
"Model: ABC123", "Features: 4K resolution, HDR support"]
product_description                                              =
generate_product_description(product_attributes)
print("Generated Product Description:", product_description)
```

Explanation:
- We load a pre-trained GPT-2 language model and tokenizer from the Hugging Face Transformers library.
- The `generate_product_description` function takes product attributes as input and generates a product description using the GPT-2 model.
- We concatenate the input product attributes into a single string and tokenize it using the tokenizer.
- We generate a product description using the GPT-2 model, specifying the maximum length of the generated text and the temperature parameter for controlling randomness in the generation process.
- Finally, we decode the generated description and return it as

the output.

Results:

The automated product description generation system successfully generates descriptive and persuasive product descriptions based on input product attributes. By leveraging generative AI technology, the retail company can automate the content creation process, save time and resources, and deliver consistent and engaging product descriptions to customers across its product catalog.

Conclusion:

Generative AI-powered automated product description generation offers retailers a scalable and efficient solution for creating engaging and informative product content. By leveraging NLP and deep learning techniques, retailers can automate the process of generating product descriptions, improve consistency, and enhance customer engagement. Automated product description generation represents a significant opportunity for retailers to streamline content creation, improve efficiency, and deliver compelling product experiences to customers in today's competitive retail landscape.

CASE STUDY: PERSONALIZED FASHION DESIGN RECOMMENDATIONS WITH GENERATIVE AI IN RETAIL

Introduction:
In the fashion retail industry, offering personalized fashion design recommendations is crucial for enhancing customer satisfaction and driving sales. However, providing customized design suggestions tailored to individual preferences and style preferences can be challenging for retailers. Generative AI offers a solution by analyzing customer data and generating personalized fashion design recommendations based on individual tastes, preferences, and body measurements. In this case study, we'll explore how a fictional fashion retail company implements personalized fashion design recommendations using generative AI technology.

Problem Statement:
The fashion retail company wants to offer personalized fashion design recommendations to its customers to enhance their shopping experience and increase conversion rates.

However, recommending suitable fashion designs that align with individual preferences, body types, and style preferences presents a significant challenge. The company seeks a solution to analyze customer data and generate personalized fashion design recommendations that resonate with each customer's unique preferences and characteristics.

Solution:
The fashion retail company decides to implement a personalized fashion design recommendation system powered by generative AI technology. The solution will leverage machine learning algorithms to analyze customer data, including past purchases, browsing behavior, style preferences, and body measurements, to generate personalized fashion design recommendations. By combining data-driven insights with generative AI techniques, the company aims to deliver tailored fashion design suggestions that cater to each customer's individual tastes and preferences.

Implementation:
We'll implement a personalized fashion design recommendation system using Python, TensorFlow, and deep learning techniques. The system will use customer data to train a generative AI model that generates personalized fashion design recommendations based on individual preferences and characteristics.

Python Code:
```python
import pandas as pd
import numpy as np
from sklearn.model_selection import train_test_split
from sklearn.preprocessing import StandardScaler
from tensorflow.keras.models import Sequential
from tensorflow.keras.layers import Dense
from tensorflow.keras.optimizers import Adam

# Load customer data (including past purchases, browsing
```

```
behavior, and body measurements)
customer_data = pd.read_csv("customer_data.csv")

# Preprocess data (dummy implementation)
# Convert categorical features to numerical encoding
customer_data        =        pd.get_dummies(customer_data,
columns=["style_preference", "body_type"])

# Split data into features (X) and target variable (y)
X        =        customer_data.drop(columns=["customer_id",
"fashion_design"])
y = customer_data["fashion_design"]

# Normalize feature data
scaler = StandardScaler()
X_scaled = scaler.fit_transform(X)

# Split data into training and test sets
X_train, X_test, y_train, y_test = train_test_split(X_scaled, y,
test_size=0.2, random_state=42)

# Define neural network model architecture
model = Sequential([
    Dense(64,                                    activation='relu',
input_shape=(X_train.shape[1],)),
    Dense(32, activation='relu'),
    Dense(1, activation='sigmoid')
])

# Compile model
model.compile(optimizer=Adam(learning_rate=0.001),
loss='binary_crossentropy', metrics=['accuracy'])

# Train model
model.fit(X_train,    y_train,    epochs=10,    batch_size=32,
validation_data=(X_test, y_test))

# Generate personalized fashion design recommendations
def
```

```
generate_fashion_design_recommendations(customer_feature
s):
    # Predict fashion design recommendation using trained
neural network model
    recommendation_probability                              =
model.predict(customer_features)
    return recommendation_probability

# Example usage
customer_features = np.array([[0, 1, 0, 0, 1, 0, 1, 0, 0]]) # Example
customer features (e.g., style preferences, body measurements)
recommendation_probability                                 =
generate_fashion_design_recommendations(customer_feature
s)
print("Fashion    Design    Recommendation    Probability:",
recommendation_probability)
` ` `
```

Explanation:
- We load customer data, including past purchases, browsing
behavior, style preferences, and body measurements, from a CSV
file.
- We preprocess the data by converting categorical features to
numerical encoding and normalizing feature data.
- We split the data into training and test sets for model training
and evaluation.
- We define a neural network model architecture using
TensorFlow's Keras API with three dense layers.
- We compile and train the neural network model using binary
crossentropy loss and Adam optimizer.
- The `generate_fashion_design_recommendations` function
takes customer features as input and generates personalized
fashion design recommendations using the trained neural
network model.
- We demonstrate an example usage of the function by providing
sample customer features and obtaining a recommendation

probability.

Results:

The personalized fashion design recommendation system successfully generates personalized recommendations based on customer features, including style preferences and body measurements. By leveraging generative AI technology, the fashion retail company can offer tailored fashion design suggestions that align with each customer's individual tastes and characteristics, enhancing the overall shopping experience and driving customer satisfaction and loyalty.

Conclusion:

Generative AI-powered personalized fashion design recommendations offer retailers a powerful solution for delivering customized fashion design suggestions to customers. By analyzing customer data and leveraging deep learning techniques, retailers can generate personalized fashion design recommendations that resonate with each customer's unique preferences and characteristics. Personalized fashion design recommendations represent a significant opportunity for retailers to enhance the shopping experience, increase customer satisfaction, and drive business growth in the competitive fashion retail industry.

CASE STUDY: VIRTUAL INTERIOR DESIGN CONSULTATION WITH GENERATIVE AI IN RETAIL

Introduction:
In the home decor retail industry, providing personalized interior design consultations is essential for helping customers visualize and plan their living spaces. However, offering in-person consultations can be logistically challenging and time-consuming. Generative AI offers a solution by enabling retailers to provide virtual interior design consultations that simulate real-world design scenarios and help customers make informed decisions about their home decor purchases. In this case study, we'll explore how a fictional home decor retail company implements virtual interior design consultations using generative AI technology.

Problem Statement:
The home decor retail company wants to offer personalized interior design consultations to its customers to enhance their shopping experience and increase sales. However, conducting in-person consultations with interior design experts for each customer is impractical and costly. The company seeks a

solution to provide virtual interior design consultations that allow customers to visualize and customize their living spaces with home decor products.

Solution:
The home decor retail company decides to implement a virtual interior design consultation system powered by generative AI technology. The solution will leverage computer vision, augmented reality (AR), and deep learning techniques to analyze customer's living spaces, recommend home decor products, and simulate design scenarios virtually. By combining data-driven insights with generative AI capabilities, the company aims to provide personalized interior design consultations that help customers make informed decisions about their home decor purchases.

Implementation:
We'll implement a virtual interior design consultation system using Python, TensorFlow, and ARKit (for iOS) or ARCore (for Android) for augmented reality functionalities. The system will use customer's room images and preferences to recommend home decor products and visualize design scenarios virtually.

Python Code (Partial Implementation):
```python
import numpy as np
import tensorflow as tf
from tensorflow.keras.models import load_model
import cv2

# Load pre-trained generative AI model for virtual interior design
model = load_model("virtual_interior_design_model.h5")

# Function to generate virtual interior design visualization
def         generate_interior_design_visualization(room_image, selected_products):
    # Preprocess room image (resize, normalize, etc.)
```

```
    # Dummy implementation
    resized_image = cv2.resize(room_image, (256, 256))
    normalized_image = resized_image / 255.0

    # Preprocess selected products data (e.g., product IDs,
positions, orientations)
    # Dummy implementation
    processed_products_data                              =
preprocess_selected_products(selected_products)

    # Generate virtual interior design visualization using
generative AI model
    visualization        =        model.predict([normalized_image,
processed_products_data])

    return visualization

# Function to display virtual interior design visualization
def display_interior_design_visualization(visualization):
    # Display visualization using ARKit or ARCore for augmented
reality functionalities
    # Dummy implementation
    pass

# Example usage
room_image = cv2.imread("room_image.jpg")
selected_products = [{"product_id": "001", "position": [100, 200],
"orientation": 45},
                {"product_id": "002", "position": [300, 150],
"orientation": 90}]
visualization                                            =
generate_interior_design_visualization(room_image,
selected_products)
display_interior_design_visualization(visualization)
` ` `
```

Explanation:
- We load a pre-trained generative AI model for virtual interior

design that takes room images and selected products data as input and generates virtual interior design visualizations.

- The `generate_interior_design_visualization` function preprocesses the room image and selected products data and generates a virtual interior design visualization using the generative AI model.

- The `display_interior_design_visualization` function displays the virtual interior design visualization using ARKit or ARCore for augmented reality functionalities, allowing customers to visualize home decor products in their living spaces.

Results:

The virtual interior design consultation system successfully generates virtual interior design visualizations based on customer's room images and selected home decor products. By leveraging generative AI technology and augmented reality functionalities, the home decor retail company can provide personalized interior design consultations that help customers visualize and customize their living spaces with home decor products, enhancing the overall shopping experience and driving sales.

Conclusion:

Generative AI-powered virtual interior design consultations offer retailers a scalable and immersive solution for providing personalized interior design services to customers. By leveraging computer vision, augmented reality, and deep learning techniques, retailers can simulate design scenarios virtually and help customers make informed decisions about their home decor purchases. Virtual interior design consultations represent a significant opportunity for retailers to differentiate themselves, enhance customer engagement, and drive sales in the competitive home decor retail industry.

CASE STUDY: CUSTOMIZED PRODUCT DESIGN WITH GENERATIVE AI IN RETAIL

Introduction:
In the retail industry, offering customized products tailored to individual preferences is increasingly important for driving customer satisfaction and loyalty. However, traditional methods of customizing products can be time-consuming and costly, often requiring manual intervention and expertise. Generative AI offers a solution by automating the process of customizing product designs based on customer input and preferences. In this case study, we'll explore how a fictional retail company implements customized product design using generative AI technology.

Problem Statement:
The retail company aims to offer customized product design services to its customers, allowing them to personalize products according to their preferences, such as color, pattern, and style. However, manually customizing product designs for each customer is impractical and inefficient. The company seeks a solution to automate the customization process and generate

personalized product designs quickly and efficiently.

Solution:
The retail company decides to implement a customized product design system powered by generative AI technology. The solution will leverage machine learning algorithms to analyze customer input and preferences and generate customized product designs automatically. By combining customer data with generative AI capabilities, the company aims to offer a seamless and efficient way for customers to personalize products according to their preferences.

Implementation:
We'll implement a customized product design system using Python, TensorFlow, and generative adversarial networks (GANs). The system will use customer input and preferences to train a GAN model that generates customized product designs based on individual preferences.

Python Code (Partial Implementation):
```python
import numpy as np
import tensorflow as tf
from tensorflow.keras.models import Sequential
from tensorflow.keras.layers import Dense, Reshape, Conv2D, Conv2DTranspose, LeakyReLU, Flatten
from tensorflow.keras.optimizers import Adam

# Define GAN model architecture for customized product design
def build_generator(latent_dim, output_shape):
    model = Sequential([
        Dense(128, input_dim=latent_dim),
        LeakyReLU(alpha=0.2),
        Dense(256),
        LeakyReLU(alpha=0.2),
        Dense(512),
        LeakyReLU(alpha=0.2),
```

```
        Dense(np.prod(output_shape), activation='sigmoid'),
        Reshape(output_shape)
    ])
    return model

def build_discriminator(input_shape):
    model = Sequential([
        Flatten(input_shape=input_shape),
        Dense(512),
        LeakyReLU(alpha=0.2),
        Dense(256),
        LeakyReLU(alpha=0.2),
        Dense(1, activation='sigmoid')
    ])
    return model

def build_gan(generator, discriminator):
    discriminator.trainable = False
    model = Sequential([
        generator,
        discriminator
    ])
    return model

# Define functions for training GAN model
def    train_gan(generator,    discriminator,    gan,    X_train,
latent_dim, n_epochs, batch_size):
    for epoch in range(n_epochs):
        for i in range(0, X_train.shape[0], batch_size):
            # Train discriminator
            noise   =   np.random.normal(0,   1,   (batch_size,
latent_dim))
            generated_images = generator.predict(noise)
            real_images = X_train[i:i+batch_size]
            X = np.concatenate([real_images, generated_images])
            y    =    np.concatenate([np.ones((batch_size,    1)),
np.zeros((batch_size, 1))])
```

```python
        discriminator_loss = discriminator.train_on_batch(X,
y)

        # Train generator
        noise = np.random.normal(0, 1, (batch_size,
latent_dim))
        y = np.ones((batch_size, 1))
        generator_loss = gan.train_on_batch(noise, y)

    print(f"Epoch {epoch+1}/{n_epochs}, Discriminator Loss:
{discriminator_loss}, Generator Loss: {generator_loss}")

# Load and preprocess customer input and preferences data
(dummy implementation)
# X_train = ...
# Y_train = ...

# Define parameters
latent_dim = 100
output_shape = (28, 28, 1)
n_epochs = 100
batch_size = 64

# Build and compile GAN model
generator = build_generator(latent_dim, output_shape)
discriminator = build_discriminator(output_shape)
discriminator.compile(optimizer=Adam(learning_rate=0.0002)
, loss='binary_crossentropy', metrics=['accuracy'])
gan = build_gan(generator, discriminator)
gan.compile(optimizer=Adam(learning_rate=0.0002),
loss='binary_crossentropy', metrics=['accuracy'])

# Train GAN model
train_gan(generator, discriminator, gan, X_train, latent_dim,
n_epochs, batch_size)

# Generate customized product design
def             generate_customized_product_design(generator,
latent_dim):
```

```
noise = np.random.normal(0, 1, (1, latent_dim))
customized_design = generator.predict(noise)
return customized_design

# Example usage
customized_product_design                              =
generate_customized_product_design(generator, latent_dim)
` ` `
```

Explanation:
- We define the architecture of the generator and discriminator networks for the GAN model.
- We build the GAN model by combining the generator and discriminator networks.
- We define functions for training the GAN model and generating customized product designs.
- We load and preprocess customer input and preferences data (not shown) to train the GAN model.
- We train the GAN model using the training data.
- Finally, we generate customized product designs using the trained generator network.

Results:
The customized product design system successfully generates personalized product designs based on customer input and preferences. By leveraging generative AI technology and GANs, the retail company can automate the customization process and offer customers a seamless way to personalize products according to their preferences, driving customer satisfaction and loyalty.

Conclusion:
Generative AI-powered customized product design offers retailers a scalable and efficient solution for providing personalized products to customers. By leveraging machine learning algorithms and GANs, retailers can automate the customization process and generate customized product

designs that align with individual preferences. Customized product design represents a significant opportunity for retailers to differentiate themselves, enhance customer satisfaction, and drive sales in the competitive retail industry.

CASE STUDY: VIRTUAL FITTING ROOM EXPERIENCE WITH GENERATIVE AI IN RETAIL

Introduction:
In the fashion retail industry, providing a seamless and immersive shopping experience is essential for attracting and retaining customers. Virtual fitting room experiences allow customers to try on clothes virtually, enabling them to visualize how different outfits look on them without physically trying them on. Generative AI technology can enhance virtual fitting room experiences by accurately simulating clothing on customers' bodies, leading to increased customer engagement and satisfaction. In this case study, we'll explore how a fictional fashion retail company implements a virtual fitting room experience using generative AI technology.

Problem Statement:
The fashion retail company aims to offer a virtual fitting room experience to its customers, allowing them to try on clothes virtually and make informed purchasing decisions. However, creating a realistic virtual fitting room experience that accurately simulates clothing on customers' bodies presents

a significant challenge. The company seeks a solution to implement a virtual fitting room experience that provides an immersive and realistic try-on experience, leading to increased customer engagement and sales.

Solution:
The fashion retail company decides to implement a virtual fitting room experience powered by generative AI technology. The solution will leverage computer vision and deep learning techniques to analyze customer's body measurements and clothing items and generate realistic virtual try-on experiences. By combining data-driven insights with generative AI capabilities, the company aims to provide customers with a seamless and immersive try-on experience that replicates the feeling of trying on clothes in a physical store.

Implementation:
We'll implement a virtual fitting room experience using Python, TensorFlow, and OpenCV for computer vision functionalities. The system will use a pre-trained generative AI model to simulate clothing on customers' bodies in real-time.

Python Code (Partial Implementation):

```python
import cv2
import numpy as np
from tensorflow.keras.models import load_model

# Load pre-trained generative AI model for virtual fitting room
model = load_model("virtual_fitting_room_model.h5")

# Function to generate virtual try-on result
def generate_virtual_try_on_result(customer_image, clothing_image):
    # Preprocess customer image (resize, normalize, etc.)
    # Dummy implementation
    resized_customer_image = cv2.resize(customer_image, (256, 256))
```

```
    normalized_customer_image = resized_customer_image /
255.0

    # Preprocess clothing image (resize, normalize, etc.)
    # Dummy implementation
    resized_clothing_image = cv2.resize(clothing_image, (256,
256))
    normalized_clothing_image = resized_clothing_image /
255.0

    # Generate virtual try-on result using generative AI model
    virtual_try_on_result                                  =
model.predict([normalized_customer_image,
normalized_clothing_image])

    return virtual_try_on_result

# Function to display virtual try-on result
def            display_virtual_try_on_result(customer_image,
virtual_try_on_result):
    # Display virtual try-on result using OpenCV
    # Dummy implementation
    cv2.imshow("Virtual Try-On", virtual_try_on_result)
    cv2.waitKey(0)
    cv2.destroyAllWindows()

# Example usage
customer_image = cv2.imread("customer_image.jpg")
clothing_image = cv2.imread("clothing_image.jpg")
virtual_try_on_result                                  =
generate_virtual_try_on_result(customer_image,
clothing_image)
display_virtual_try_on_result(customer_image,
virtual_try_on_result)
```

Explanation:
- We load a pre-trained generative AI model for virtual fitting

room that takes customer images and clothing images as input and generates virtual try-on results.

- The `generate_virtual_try_on_result` function preprocesses customer images and clothing images, generates virtual try-on results using the generative AI model, and returns the results.

- The `display_virtual_try_on_result` function displays the virtual try-on results using OpenCV for real-time visualization.

Results:

The virtual fitting room experience successfully generates realistic virtual try-on results, allowing customers to visualize how different clothing items look on them in real-time. By leveraging generative AI technology, the fashion retail company can provide customers with an immersive and engaging try-on experience that replicates the feeling of trying on clothes in a physical store, leading to increased customer satisfaction and sales.

Conclusion:

Generative AI-powered virtual fitting room experiences offer retailers a scalable and immersive solution for providing customers with an engaging and realistic try-on experience. By leveraging computer vision and deep learning techniques, retailers can simulate clothing on customers' bodies virtually, allowing them to visualize how different outfits look on them before making a purchase. Virtual fitting room experiences represent a significant opportunity for retailers to enhance customer engagement, increase sales, and differentiate themselves in the competitive fashion retail industry.

CASE STUDY: CUSTOMIZED JEWELRY DESIGN WITH GENERATIVE AI IN RETAIL

Introduction:
In the jewelry retail industry, offering customized jewelry designs is a growing trend that allows customers to create unique pieces tailored to their preferences. However, designing custom jewelry can be complex and time-consuming, often requiring specialized expertise and resources. Generative AI offers a solution by automating the process of generating customized jewelry designs based on customer input and preferences. In this case study, we'll explore how a fictional jewelry retail company implements customized jewelry design using generative AI technology.

Problem Statement:
The jewelry retail company aims to offer customized jewelry design services to its customers, allowing them to design personalized pieces according to their preferences, such as gemstone selection, metal type, and design style. However, manually designing custom jewelry for each customer is impractical and inefficient. The company seeks a solution to

automate the customization process and generate personalized jewelry designs quickly and efficiently.

Solution:
The jewelry retail company decides to implement a customized jewelry design system powered by generative AI technology. The solution will leverage machine learning algorithms to analyze customer input and preferences and generate customized jewelry designs automatically. By combining customer data with generative AI capabilities, the company aims to provide customers with a seamless and efficient way to design personalized jewelry pieces that reflect their individual style and preferences.

Implementation:
We'll implement a customized jewelry design system using Python, TensorFlow, and generative adversarial networks (GANs). The system will use customer input and preferences to train a GAN model that generates customized jewelry designs based on individual preferences.

Python Code (Partial Implementation):

```python
import numpy as np
import tensorflow as tf
from tensorflow.keras.models import Sequential
from tensorflow.keras.layers import Dense, Reshape, Conv2D, Conv2DTranspose, LeakyReLU, Flatten
from tensorflow.keras.optimizers import Adam

# Define GAN model architecture for customized jewelry design
def build_generator(latent_dim, output_shape):
    model = Sequential([
        Dense(128, input_dim=latent_dim),
        LeakyReLU(alpha=0.2),
        Dense(256),
        LeakyReLU(alpha=0.2),
```

```python
        Dense(512),
        LeakyReLU(alpha=0.2),
        Dense(np.prod(output_shape), activation='sigmoid'),
        Reshape(output_shape)
    ])
    return model

def build_discriminator(input_shape):
    model = Sequential([
        Flatten(input_shape=input_shape),
        Dense(512),
        LeakyReLU(alpha=0.2),
        Dense(256),
        LeakyReLU(alpha=0.2),
        Dense(1, activation='sigmoid')
    ])
    return model

def build_gan(generator, discriminator):
    discriminator.trainable = False
    model = Sequential([
        generator,
        discriminator
    ])
    return model

# Define functions for training GAN model
def train_gan(generator, discriminator, gan, X_train,
latent_dim, n_epochs, batch_size):
    for epoch in range(n_epochs):
        for i in range(0, X_train.shape[0], batch_size):
            # Train discriminator
            noise = np.random.normal(0, 1, (batch_size,
latent_dim))
            generated_images = generator.predict(noise)
            real_images = X_train[i:i+batch_size]
            X = np.concatenate([real_images, generated_images])
```

```
        y    =    np.concatenate([np.ones((batch_size,    1)),
np.zeros((batch_size, 1))])
        discriminator_loss = discriminator.train_on_batch(X,
y)

        # Train generator
        noise   =   np.random.normal(0,   1,   (batch_size,
latent_dim))
        y = np.ones((batch_size, 1))
        generator_loss = gan.train_on_batch(noise, y)

    print(f"Epoch {epoch+1}/{n_epochs}, Discriminator Loss:
{discriminator_loss}, Generator Loss: {generator_loss}")

# Load and preprocess customer input and preferences data
(dummy implementation)
# X_train = ...
# Y_train = ...

# Define parameters
latent_dim = 100
output_shape = (28, 28, 1)
n_epochs = 100
batch_size = 64

# Build and compile GAN model
generator = build_generator(latent_dim, output_shape)
discriminator = build_discriminator(output_shape)
discriminator.compile(optimizer=Adam(learning_rate=0.0002)
, loss='binary_crossentropy', metrics=['accuracy'])
gan = build_gan(generator, discriminator)
gan.compile(optimizer=Adam(learning_rate=0.0002),
loss='binary_crossentropy', metrics=['accuracy'])

# Train GAN model
train_gan(generator, discriminator, gan, X_train, latent_dim,
n_epochs, batch_size)

# Generate customized jewelry design
```

```
def         generate_customized_jewelry_design(generator,
latent_dim):
    noise = np.random.normal(0, 1, (1, latent_dim))
    customized_design = generator.predict(noise)
    return customized_design

# Example usage
customized_jewelry_design                        =
generate_customized_jewelry_design(generator, latent_dim)
```

Explanation:
- We define the architecture of the generator and discriminator networks for the GAN model.
- We build the GAN model by combining the generator and discriminator networks.
- We define functions for training the GAN model and generating customized jewelry

designs.
- We load and preprocess customer input and preferences data (not shown) to train the GAN model.
- We train the GAN model using the training data.
- Finally, we generate customized jewelry designs using the trained generator network.

Results:
The customized jewelry design system successfully generates personalized jewelry designs based on customer input and preferences. By leveraging generative AI technology and GANs, the jewelry retail company can automate the customization process and offer customers a seamless way to design unique jewelry pieces that reflect their individual style and preferences, leading to increased customer satisfaction and sales.

Conclusion:
Generative AI-powered customized jewelry design offers retailers a scalable and efficient solution for providing

customers with personalized jewelry pieces. By leveraging machine learning algorithms and GANs, retailers can automate the customization process and generate customized jewelry designs that align with individual preferences. Customized jewelry design represents a significant opportunity for retailers to differentiate themselves, enhance customer satisfaction, and drive sales in the competitive jewelry retail industry.